解析亚里士多德
《尼各马可伦理学》

AN ANALYSIS OF
ARISTOTLE'S
NICOMACHEAN
ETHICS

Giovanni Gellera　　Jon W. Thompson ◎ 著
韩晓龙 ◎ 译

目 录

引 言 1
亚里士多德其人 2
《形而上学》的主要内容 3
《形而上学》的学术价值 5

第一部分：学术概说 9
1. 亚里士多德与形而上学 10
2. 学术背景 15
3. 主导问题 19
4. 作者及名辨 24

第二部分：学术回顾 29
5. 柏拉图主义 30
6. 亚维柏主义 35
7. 历史回顾续 40
8. 著作成因 45

第三部分：学术影响 51
9. 最初之影响 52
10. 后续影响续 56
11. 当代的影响 62
12. 未来的影响 68

术语表 73
人名表 78

CONTENTS

WAYS IN TO THE TEXT	85
Who Was Aristotle?	86
What Does *Nicomachean Ethics* Say?	87
Why Does *Nicomachean Ethics* Matter?	90
SECTION 1: INFLUENCES	93
Module 1: The Author and the Historical Context	94
Module 2: Academic Context	99
Module 3: The Problem	104
Module 4: The Author's Contribution	109
SECTION 2: IDEAS	115
Module 5: Main Ideas	116
Module 6: Secondary Ideas	122
Module 7: Achievement	128
Module 8: Place in the Author's Work	134
SECTION 3: IMPACT	141
Module 9: The First Responses	142
Module 10: The Evolving Debate	146
Module 11: Impact and Influence Today	153
Module 12: Where Next?	159
Glossary of Terms	164
People Mentioned in the Text	171
Works Cited	175

引 言

要 点

- 亚里士多德于公元前 384 年出生于希腊斯塔吉拉,是史上最伟大的哲学家*之一。
- 《尼各马可伦理学》创作于公元前 335 年至公元前 322 年。在书中,亚里士多德提出"幸福就是至高的善"的观点,并且提出真正的幸福的获取要依靠伦理上善的行为(伦理学*是哲学*的分支之一,讨论人应该如何生活的问题)。
- 《尼各马可伦理学》中,亚里士多德强调伦理上善的行为来自道德德性*和理智德性(德性指性格和行为的倾向)。

亚里士多德其人

亚里士多德,《尼各马可伦理学》(创作于公元前 335 年至公元前 322 年)的作者,古希腊哲学家,有史以来最为著名的思想家之一。他出生于马其顿一个叫斯塔吉拉的小镇(马其顿是古典希腊时期希腊北部的一个王国)。亚里士多德的父亲是一位医生,名为尼各马可,母亲名叫菲俄斯蒂斯。亚里士多德 18 岁时,前往希腊世界的学习中心雅典,跟随伟大的哲学家柏拉图*学习哲学。他求学的地方,就是柏拉图创立的柏拉图学园*,是著名的哲学学习的中心,亚里士多德在此一直学习到公元前 348 年。公元前 343 年,他成为年轻的亚历山大大帝*的老师。亚历山大大帝是马其顿国王腓力二世的儿子,后来成为军事领袖,统治庞大的帝国(其中包含了希腊)。

亚里士多德返回雅典后,于公元前 335 年创办了自己的学校吕克昂*,来教育杰出的年轻人。因为学园附近有可供散步的圆形柱廊，亚里士多德和他的追随者常被称作"漫步学派"*（又译"逍遥学派"）。在吕克昂任校长期间，亚里士多德向学生讲授众多科目，包括政治学、物理学、诗歌和逻辑学*（逻辑学是哲学的分支，主要研究系统、理性的推理）等。在度过了漫长而又成绩卓著的教育生涯之后，亚里士多德于公元前322年逝世于希腊埃维厄岛，享年62岁。

亚里士多德将其毕生精力奉献给了学习和探索自然，以及向学生传授知识。他之所以能成为史上最重要的思想家之一，很大程度上是因为他的现存的一部分最具影响力的、系统性的哲学著作。他还开创了两个新的学科领域：逻辑学和生物学*。亚里士多德的很多作品是关于伦理学（研究对与错的学问）的，而《尼各马可伦理学》是用他父亲的名字来命名的，是一部永恒的哲学经典。一位评论家曾经说过："亚里士多德在哲学史上具有无与伦比的重要地位——他是一位非常优秀的、至善的哲学家。"[1] 很多我们现在所认为的西方*（主要是欧洲、北美及澳大利亚—新西兰区域）的道德观念和准则，都可以追溯到《尼各马可伦理学》，追溯到亚里士多德关于幸福、德性和实践智慧的概念。

《尼各马可伦理学》的主要内容

《尼各马可伦理学》现在被认为是史上第一部伦理学专著*（系统的书面解析），但亚里士多德并未亲自出版该书，很有可能是他的一位学生根据亚里士多德于公元前335年至322年在吕克昂的教学笔记编辑而成。无论如何，这部著作对亚里士多德之后的每一个时代的道德哲学*都产生了深远的影响。（"道德哲学"是研究道德的理论和实践的哲学分支，即研究"我们应该如何生活"

这一问题。)

大多数《尼各马可伦理学》的现行版本包括10卷，其中各有章节，分卷的方法源自《尼各马可伦理学》已知的最早版本，而划分章节则是现代版本常见的做法。在引用《尼各马可伦理学》时，其引用格式包括两部分。如"X.7.1177a13-18"，此例中第一部分（"X.7"）指学者罗吉尔·克里斯普[2]翻译本的第10卷第7章，一般的引用大多只包含这一部分。第二部分（"1177a13-18"）遵照的是德国哲学家奥古斯特·伊曼努尔·贝克*于1831年所创的文本引用体系。标明了第二部分的引用格式之后，读者能在亚里士多德作品的几乎任意一个翻译本中找到文章的出处。

《尼各马可伦理学》研究"什么是好的生活"这一问题。在回答这一问题时，亚里士多德提出，好的生活就是按照人类本性的功能或者目的（希腊语：*ergon*）*生活。

在亚里士多德看来，"功能"是一个事物独一无二的、界定性的目的。比如，一把小刀的功能是切割，一个锤子的功能是敲击。亚里士多德向自己提出了一个问题："人类的功能是什么？"——换言之，人类应该做什么？

亚里士多德认为人类的最大功能是幸福（希腊语：*eudaimonia*）*，也就是要生活得好。那么幸福包含哪些内容呢？

亚里士多德认为，我们人类的功能，是由将我们与这个世界上其他事物区别开来的特征决定的，那就是理性*（人类抽象思维的能力）。作为人类，我们的理性可以运用在理论性的问题中，也可以运用在实际性的事务中。因此，我们的功能——也是我们得到幸福的关键——是通过恰当的理论理性和实践理性来实现的。

在亚里士多德看来，理论理性和实践理性的恰当运用，在于找到行为和品格的极端之间的中间道路；实践理性要求人们在面对危险时，既不能怯懦，也不能鲁莽。这两个极端之间的中道*（即应该达到的中间道路）就是勇敢的品格特征。这样的"中道"品格特征就是"德性"。亚里士多德罗列了许多德性，包括正义、勇气、节制*（即克制，通常对享乐性的活动而言），以及实践智慧等。

亚里士多德也没有忽略对理论理性的探讨。在《尼各马可伦理学》的末尾，他回到了沉思*这个话题（在他看来，沉思是对永恒真理的思考）。他认为，沉思的生活是最幸福的。在第10卷的第7至8章（X.7-8），他写道："如果说幸福是合乎德性的活动，那么我们可以合理的期待，这（指下文提到的沉思）是合乎最高的德性的……（这个）活动就是沉思。"[3]

对于《尼各马可伦理学》所涉及的社会和政治方面的核心内容，我们可以将其看作对亚里士多德的另一部关于实践问题的重要作品《政治学》的延续。在后者当中，他提出了人是"政治动物"的著名定义（《政治学》，1253a1-4）：我们的生活本质上是社会性的，我们需要其他人的陪伴以获得幸福。[4]进一步说，由个体组成的群体的目标和个体的目标是并行不悖的。因此，政治家的高尚目标应该是创造公民幸福的物质条件，正如个体的目标是获得自身幸福所必需的德性一样。

《尼各马可伦理学》的学术价值

《尼各马可伦理学》和亚里士多德的观点在哲学史上的影响力很可能是无与伦比的。牛津大学哲学教授特伦斯·欧文*曾说过："我们可以通过一条重要的线把道德哲学的历史贯穿起来，那就是去思考亚里士多德在多大程度上是正确的，以及他的继承者们对他观点的看法。"⁵ 中世纪*的思想家们把亚里士多德称为"唯一的哲学家"。时至今日，亚里士多德的观点仍然经得起时间的考验。德性伦理学*——主要研究道德品质的伦理学学派——现在是当代道德哲学的主导流派。⁶ 新西兰哲学家罗莎琳德·赫斯特豪斯*写道："德性伦理学既是伦理学的老方法，也是新方法。'老'是因为它最早可以回溯到柏拉图甚至亚里士多德的著作；'新'是因为它作为这种古老方法的复兴，是当代道德哲学领域相对近期的一个新增内容。"⁷

但是，《尼各马可伦理学》的重要性并不仅仅是对于那些从事哲学学术研究的人而言。在亚里士多德看来，哲学"始于惊奇"。⁸ 或许没有任何其他关于人类的问题比《尼各马可伦理学》所探讨的问题更令人感到惊奇了。幸福的本质是什么？人类如何才能获得幸福？而人类又为何不能获得幸福？这些普世的、具备深厚的人文关怀的问题，使得《尼各马可伦理学》拥有了经久不衰的重要价值。

最后，当我们将亚里士多德的《尼各马可伦理学》与《政治学》相提并论时，我们仍然能发现其与政治科学和社会科学中永恒的问题的关联。虽然亚里士多德创作《尼各马可伦理学》时的文化和当代全球社会的文化完全不同，但他的作品直到今天还对我们意义深远。他的伦理思想给我们现代的社会和政治的设想提供了一个参照物。可以说，亚里士多德是一位强大的对话者，在哪怕是当代世界最为紧迫的政治和经济问题上，他也能给我们提供一个截然不同的视角。⁹

1. 乔纳森·巴恩斯：《剑桥亚里士多德指南》，剑桥：剑桥大学出版社，1995 年，第 9 章．
2. 亚里士多德：《尼各马可伦理学（修订版）》，罗吉尔·克里斯普编译，剑桥：剑桥大学出版社，2014 年。
3. 亚里士多德：《尼各马可伦理学》，第 10 卷，第 7 章，1177a13—18。
4. 亚里士多德：《政治学》，特伦斯·欧文译，选自《古希腊哲学选读》，马克·科恩、帕特丽夏·柯德和 C. D. C. 里夫编，印第安纳波利斯：哈克特出版社，2005 年，1253al—4。
5. 特伦斯·欧文：《伦理学发展史》，第 1 卷，牛津：牛津大学出版社，2007 年，第 4 页。
6. 罗莎琳德·赫斯特豪斯："德性伦理学"，选自《斯坦福哲学百科词典》（2013 秋季版），登录日期 2016 年 2 月 27 日，http://plato.stanford.edu/archives/fall2013/entries/ethics-virtue/。
7. 罗莎琳德·赫斯特豪斯：《德性伦理学》，牛津：牛津大学出版社，2001 年，第 9 页。
8. 亚里士多德：《形而上学》，马克·科恩译，选自《古希腊哲学选读》，982b10—15。
9. 关于亚里士多德及其伦理学在现代所具革命性的讨论，参见保罗·布莱克利奇和凯文·奈特编：《德性与政治：阿拉斯代尔·麦金泰尔的革命性的亚里士多德哲学》，印第安纳诺特丹：圣母大学出版社，2011 年。

第一部分：学术渊源

1 作者生平与历史背景

要点

- 亚里士多德的《尼各马可伦理学》研究人类幸福的问题,是道德哲学领域的基础性著作之一。
- 跟随具有深远影响力的思想家柏拉图学习了 20 年之后,亚里士多德写出了自己开创性的著作。
- 亚里士多德是古希腊学者中的重要人物,他是军事领袖亚历山大大帝的老师。亚历山大大帝后来成为庞大帝国的统治者。

为何要读这部著作?

《尼各马可伦理学》(创作于公元前 335 年至公元前 322 年)的作者亚里士多德曾经说过,哲学"始于惊奇"[1]——这个惊奇,来自我们对物质世界、社会世界及人类个体行为世界的未解之谜的反应。

在该书中,亚里士多德探索了人类惊奇之心的最为直接的源头——人类本性和目的的问题,以及人类该如何生活的问题。阅读亚里士多德关于伦理学的这本著作的一个重要原因,是因为该著作是西方伦理学思想的奠基之作。

中世纪*(5—15 世纪)的哲学家们一般将亚里士多德称作"唯一的哲学家"。《尼各马可伦理学》是最有影响力的伦理学著作,大约每隔 10 年就会有关于它的新的重要注释出现。这使其成为西方哲学史上研究最多、影响最大的作品之一。《尼各马可伦理学》是现存的第一部系统研究人类生活的核心伦理问题的著作,这些核心伦理问题包括幸福（*eudaimonia*）是什么、如何获得幸福等。[2] 这部著作将道德哲学确立为一门学科，并极大地影响了这一领域的术语、主要观点和学科结构。

如果满足生存的基本需求是不言而喻的，那么善的生活是由什么构成的呢？亚里士多德时代人们都认为幸福是构成好的生活的要素，但是关于幸福是什么的意见并不统一。很多人将幸福看成是享乐、荣誉或者财富，而亚里士多德继承了他的老师、具有巨大影响力的哲学家柏拉图的观点，认为以上都是错误的看法。这些东西只是人们追求其他目的的手段，而所有人类行为的最根本目标，是人们在所有的活动中所真正追求的善。

《尼各马可伦理学》对每个历史时期都产生了影响。时至今日，它仍然影响着人们的哲学和政治学思想。

> "我们或许应该考虑普遍的善，彻底地讨论它的含义。"
> ——亚里士多德：《尼各马可伦理学》

作者生平

亚里士多德于公元前 384 年出生于当时的马其顿地区的斯塔吉拉小镇，位于现在希腊北部。他的父亲尼各马可是马其顿宫廷的医生。尼各马可给自己的儿子提供了他所能提供的最好的教育。他的医生身份或许对亚里士多德产生了很大的影响，使得他的哲学著作非常注重实证和科学。（"实证"是通过观察可验证的信息进行科学研究的方法。）

亚里士多德 17 岁时前往雅典，跟随柏拉图在他的柏拉图学园中学习。[3] 公元前 347 年柏拉图逝世后，他离开了雅典，并于公元前

347年至公元前343年在小亚细亚（今土耳其）和希腊东部的爱琴群岛进行生物学研究。在莱斯博斯岛生活期间，亚里士多德娶了一位名叫皮西厄斯的女子，生下一个女儿，也起名叫皮西厄斯。随后，他迁居至马其顿王廷，暂时担任亚历山大大帝的老师。亚里士多德于公元前335年回到雅典，创建了自己的哲学学校——吕克昂。该校的成员被称作"漫步学派"，得名于希腊词汇"回廊"*，指的是学院附近可供散步的走廊。亚里士多德在吕克昂创作了他的大多数著作，并在那里任教一直到公元前323年亚历山大大帝逝世。由于他与马其顿的关系众所周知，出于对反马其顿运动的恐惧，亚里士多德离开了雅典，这一次是永远地离开。他在希腊的埃维厄岛渡过了生命的最后一年，于公元前322年逝于此地。[4]

创作背景

亚里士多德的哲学生涯中最重要的阶段都是在古希腊城邦*雅典度过的。雅典是爱琴海沿岸数百个希腊城邦中最强大的一个。它历经了公元前5世纪前叶的波斯战争*和后叶的伯罗奔尼撒战争*，而这些战争冲突深刻地塑造了这个地区。雅典被认为是民主*的诞生地。在民主体制下，统治权不是掌握在任何君主或精英的手中，而是在人民的手中。但实际上，在雅典只有拥有相当财富的男性公民才有权参加政治生活。

亚里士多德时期的雅典，政治相对稳定，文化有了巨大的进步。可以说，雅典的政治稳定来自伯罗奔尼撒战争（雅典与其敌对城邦斯巴达之间的战争）之后80年间的民主制度的成功。在此期间，民主主义者和支持精英统治的公民都得到了容忍和接受，这为哲学学派的发展提供了稳定的社会基础。遗憾的是，公元前399

年，雅典陪审团判处伟大的哲学家、亚里士多德老师柏拉图的老师苏格拉底*死刑，因为他"败坏"了哲学教学。这一著名事件是公元前4世纪雅典宽容统治的一个重大例外。

雅典的文化发展在这一时期达到了最高点，一部分原因就是政治稳定。公元前4、5世纪出现了最为著名的艺术家、雕塑家、戏剧家和哲学家。正是在这样的背景下，柏拉图的阿卡德米学园和亚里士多德的吕克昂学园得以兴盛。前者对亚里士多德接受哲学教育至关重要，而后者是他发展和传授自己的哲学思想的必需条件。公元前323年亚历山大大帝去世后，雅典的形势变得对亚里士多德不利。雅典人一直对他们北方的邻居马其顿人心怀警惕，而亚历山大大帝的去世意味着他的帝国不再稳定。传说亚里士多德逃离了雅典，避免雅典因为杀死他而对哲学"犯下两次罪行"——此前苏格拉底已经在此丧生。

亚里士多德对雅典哲学遗产的贡献是巨大的，他对更广泛意义上的人类知识的贡献也同样如此。他构建了我们今天所熟知的哲学学科，[5] 他还建立了至少两项基础的科学分支：逻辑学和生物学。[6]

---

1. 亚里士多德：《形而上学》，马克·科恩译，马克·科恩、帕特丽夏·柯德和 C. D. C. 里夫编，印第安纳波利斯：哈克特出版社，2005年，982b10—15。
2. 理查德·克劳特："两种幸福概念"，《哲学评论》第88卷，1979年，第167—197页。
3. 克里斯托弗·希尔兹："亚里士多德"，选自《斯坦福哲学百科词典》（2015秋季版），登录日期2015年1月15日，http://plato.stanford.edu/archives/fall2015/entries/

aristotle/。

4. 亚里士多德传记简略版,参见乔纳森·巴恩斯:《剑桥亚里士多德指南》,剑桥:剑桥大学出版社,1995年,第1—15页。
5. 尤其重要的是他的几部著作《物理学》《论灵魂》《形而上学》,译本参见乔纳森·巴恩斯:《亚里士多德全集》,普林斯顿:普林斯顿大学出版社,1991年。
6. 乔治斯·阿纳格诺斯托普洛斯:"亚里士多德作品及思想发展史",选自《亚里士多德指南》,乔治斯·阿纳格诺斯托普洛斯编,牛津:威利—布莱克维尔出版社,2009年。

2 学术背景

要点

- 亚里士多德的《尼各马可伦理学》是道德哲学领域最重要、最具影响力的著作。
- 幸福生活由什么构成的问题,是政治家、知识分子和普通人共同关注的核心问题。
- 亚里士多德的做法是严肃地对待大众和传统对好的生活的描述,并用哲学的方法进行评判。

著作语境

亚里士多德的《尼各马可伦理学》出现在哲学史上一个非常关键的时期,对我们今天的哲学做出了巨大的贡献。当时希腊文化的很多方面都很先进——尤其是文学(诗歌、史诗、戏剧)、历史、科学(几何学、数学)、音乐和建筑——但哲学学科却没有完全确立。哲学探讨的最重要的形式,一是口头传承,其最著名的代表就是哲学家苏格拉底(亚里士多德老师柏拉图的老师),另一个是以思想家赫拉克利特*为代表的哲理诗。柏拉图是第一位以对话录(通过人物间的谈话来揭示思想的方法)的形式广泛地进行哲学书面写作的哲学家,他的对话录常常以苏格拉底为主人公。哲学逐渐从文学和诗歌当中独立出来,成为一门学科;它探讨的很多都是与文学和诗歌所探讨的相同的问题,如生命、死亡、幸福、世界的本源与本质、伦理*、灵魂不朽等,但它使用的方法更加严谨,更具系统性。

在亚里士多德之前，希腊有三个主要的哲学流派：前苏格拉底学派*（因时间在苏格拉底之前而得名）、智者学派*（周游各地的职业教师，开展关于正义、责任、幸福、公民道德等话题的公开辩论）、以柏拉图学园为核心的苏格拉底和柏拉图的哲学流派。前苏格拉底学派以探索万物本源和根本原则而著称，[1] 该流派比较著名的哲学家有赫拉克利特、巴门尼德*和恩培多克勒*。苏格拉底是第一个以问题为核心来定义哲学的。他之所以这样做，主要是针对智者学派的。智者学派对自己关于正义和美德的看法极为自信，却无法给出有力的证明。苏格拉底也探讨了很多与智者学派相同的话题，但与智者学派相反的是，他的态度是批判性的，也是非常谦虚的。

哲学史学家安东尼·佩鲁斯*认为，自苏格拉底以来，哲学出现了一次关键的转向："'伦理学'这个词汇的发明者亚里士多德说，'在苏格拉底时期，人们放弃了对自然的探究，而哲学家们转向了政治学和实用德性*的研究。'"[2] 换而言之，从前苏格拉底学派，经过智者学派，再到苏格拉底、柏拉图和亚里士多德的知识学派，哲学经历了从推测万物本源规则到探讨伦理生活的转向。

> "现在我们大都认为将哲学的这一分支学科叫做'伦理学'（有时也称作'道德哲学'）是理所当然的，但我们必须不断地提醒自己记住：这种学科的划分方法是由人创造出来的，而亚里士多德就是它的创造者之一。"
> ——理查德·克劳特：《布莱克维尔〈尼各马可伦理学〉指南》

学科概览

在亚里士多德之前，柏拉图的《理想国》是道德哲学领域最为重要的著作。在柏拉图的大多数对话录中,都是从苏格拉底口中说出最为有趣的观点。因此,人们经常很难判断哪些是源自于苏格拉底的观点,哪些是他的学生柏拉图的首创。在《理想国》中,柏拉图第一次通过描述理想社会中的美德的方法,探讨了个人的美德。他把这个理想当中的社会划分为统治者阶层、士兵阶层和市民阶层。在一个秩序井然的城邦当中,不同阶层的人对应不同的美德发挥各自的作用:城邦的统治者必须拥有智慧(*sophia*)*;士兵,也就是城邦的保护者,必须拥有勇气(*andreia*)*;而每个阶层的成员都应具备节制(*sophrosune*)*和正义(*dikaiosune*)*。在柏拉图看来,个人是城邦的缩影,也应具备正义、勇敢、智慧和节制的品质。柏拉图预先提出了亚里士多德"四大美德"的观点。而且,他像亚里士多德一样,强调智慧在统领城邦和个人灵魂中的重要作用。因为智慧统帅个体,也统帅整个城邦,智慧将理想的社会和美德统一起来。

学术渊源

尽管亚里士多德建立了自己的哲学路径(包括术语、方法、学科划分等),但柏拉图和柏拉图学园对亚里士多德的影响是非常巨大的。柏拉图建立了阿卡德米,即柏拉图学园。它是西方世界*第一所进行理论研究的学校,当时很多最具天赋的研究者都与它有关。柏拉图继承了苏格拉底的方法,经常分析和批评一些当时最为常见的观点——即在他的对话录中由智者们提出的观点。亚里士多德在阿卡德米学习和任教直到柏拉图逝世,前后共20余年时间。因此,应该说他借鉴了苏格拉底和柏拉图的方法,特别是在《尼各马可伦理学》和《政治学》当中更是如此。哲学史学家特伦斯·欧文*确认了这一点:"亚里士多德继承了苏格拉底式的传统,批判性地审视常见的道德信仰,以便解决由此产生的困惑和难题。在柏拉图早期的对话录中,苏格拉底通过系统地诘问常见的观点,从而提出了这些难题。"[3]

当然,亚里士多德在他随后的学术生涯中发展出的独特而又迥异的观点,与上面提到的这一点也并不矛盾。经过了这样的发展,亚里士多德在《尼各马可伦理学》中批判性地讨论了柏拉图学园中的其他成员的理论,特别是柏拉图和天文学家、数学家欧多克索斯*,以及柏拉图的外甥、哲学家斯珀西波斯*等的观点。因此,在形成那些与他的老师和同僚迥然相异的观点时,亚里士多德经常与柏拉图学园的前任同事们争论,并因此收获颇丰。他还从前苏格拉底学派、柏拉图、苏格拉底、智者学派以及当时的诗歌和戏剧当中引用例子和语录。

---

1. 亚历山大·莫雷拉托斯编:《前苏格拉底学派:评论集》,新泽西普林斯顿:普林斯顿大学出版社,1993年。
2. 安东尼·佩鲁斯:《古希腊哲学史词典》,马里兰州拉汉姆:稻草人出版社,2007年,第108页。
3. 特伦斯·欧文:《伦理学发展史》,第1卷,牛津:牛津大学出版社,2007年,第2页。

3 主导命题

要点

- 古代道德哲学家们想要回答"什么是幸福"这个问题。
- 在亚里士多德的时代,普通人常常把钱财和享乐看作幸福,政治家把荣誉当成幸福,而很多哲学家认为,幸福是灵魂的一种状态。
- 亚里士多德不认同把幸福看作一种灵魂状态的观点。在他看来,幸福是合乎道德德性和理智德性的行为。

核心问题

在《尼各马可伦理学》的开头,亚里士多德提出一个观点:"每一种技能,每一次探寻,每一个行为和每一次理智的选择,都是以某种善为目的的;因此,善可以被恰当地描述为万物的目的。"[1] 据此,亚里士多德直接、明确地提出了这部著作的核心问题:什么是人类最高的善?

亚里士多德假设人类的行为一定是以某种事物为目标的,而所有人类行为最根本的目标一定是与人的本质相一致的。在回答"什么是幸福"的问题的过程中,有两样事物指引着亚里士多德,它们分别是有声望的观点(*endoxa*)*(又译"公认观点")和可观察到的现象(*phainomena*)*。作为亚里士多德哲学的一般方法,他试图在公认观点和个人日常经验中找到一致之处。[2]

在《尼各马可伦理学》第 1 卷第 4—5 章(I.4—5),亚里士多德承认有一种普遍的共识——人类追求的最高的善就是 *eudaimonia*,即幸福或者兴盛。需要指出的是,在古代社会,人们认为幸福是一种客观的状态，而不仅仅是一种主观的体验。在这一点上，所有的古代理论和我们现代对于"幸福"的用法都是不一样的——也就是说，它们把幸福看作是一种独立于我们感知之外的状态，而不是我们可以通过感觉来定义的事物。尽管亚里士多德同意柏拉图和普通民众的看法，认为幸福是至善，而且肯定是客观的，但是他也发现关于"幸福由什么构成"的问题有很大的争议。如他所言："他们对幸福的实质概念各执一词，民众和哲学家的解释截然不同。"3

亚里士多德吸收了关于什么是至善的意见分歧，发展出一种全新的关于至善本质的观点。他认为，幸福是一种行为，而不是一种存在的状态。它是完整的生活当中"合乎德性的灵魂的活动"。4

> "我认为，大多数人会赞同（最高的善的）叫法，因为民众和智者都将其称为幸福，认为幸福就等同于生活得好和行动得好。他们对于幸福的实质概念看法不一。"
> ——亚里士多德：《尼各马可伦理学》

参与者

柏拉图在《理想国》和《斐利布斯篇》*中提出，灵魂拥有的美德是幸福的充足条件。他主要把人的善看作一种存在的状态，而不是一种行为。对他而言，美德是灵魂所拥有的品格特征，永远不会被外部环境剥夺。道德的人永远是道德的，不论他或她是否有机会将这些美德表现出来。苏格拉底和柏拉图把美德比作一种技艺。工匠是否喜欢他的工作并不重要：只要产品是好的，他的技艺就是好的。

柏拉图在《理想国》中提出，如果儿童想要具备能够创造幸福的道德品质，必须接受严格的教育：因为对儿童和年轻人来说，享乐的吸引力和对痛苦的恐惧是难以避免的，所以他们需要外部的权威（比如老师和家长）指导他们的行为，教会他们美德。[5] 最后，普通人的观点是，幸福不是由美德本身构成，而是由一些外部的善构成的——比如财富、名誉、享乐等。

当时的论战

在《尼各马可伦理学》中，亚里士多德以思考"有声望的"观点（又译"公认观点"）为开端。[6] 在仔细、具体地分析了其他人（包括哲学家、圣人、诗人等）的观点之后，他提出了自己的理论。尽管很明显的是，柏拉图和他的老师苏格拉底对亚里士多德的影响最为深远，但是，亚里士多德似乎是以柏拉图的观点为依托，发展出了自己的理论最关键的主题。同时，亚里士多德也同样关注普通人对幸福的看法。

就幸福的本质而言，亚里士多德认同柏拉图的观点，认为最好的生活是以美德为核心的。但是他们的理解也有非常重大的差异。与柏拉图相反的是，亚里士多德认为对于幸福而言，美德是必须的，但并不足够；如果说一个内心道德但却生活极度贫困的人是幸福的，那是非常荒谬的。亚里士多德吸收了认为财富和荣誉对幸福有一定重要性的普遍观点，提出德性的行为和沉思体现最完整的幸福生活。他还承认一定程度的财富和健康对于这种幸福生活是必须的。

亚里士多德还发展了柏拉图对于美德和享乐的关系的理解。在《尼各马可伦理学》中，他继承了柏拉图"享乐不可能是至高的善"

的观点,指出"享乐不是善,因为善不会因为任何加诸其上的事物而变得更值得选择"。[7] 根据亚里士多德和柏拉图的观点,纯粹享乐的生活可以通过理性来改善,并以理性为特征——因此享乐不可能是最高的善,因为最高的善是不能被进一步改善的。但是,亚里士多德认为美德的最高发展将会意味着具有美德的人从自身的道德行为中获得享乐。所以,一个人勉强地做好事,说明他并不是完全道德的[8]——这是亚里士多德对柏拉图观点的一个细微的调整。

在伦理学*中,亚里士多德和柏拉图之间还有一个重要的差异。柏拉图认为,人的每一个行为都是以"善的形式"为目标的。这是柏拉图的一个抽象概念,它把所有我们称之为"善"的事物统一起来,比如一个好人、优秀的智力、精湛的箭术等等。而亚里士多德虽然承认这种理解有一定的吸引力,他从根本上却是持反对意见的。他以荣誉、实践智慧和享乐等作为例子,认为不存在那种所有好的事物都可以共同享有的"善的形式"。[9] 因此,伦理学并不需要关于抽象的"善的形式"的理论知识,只需要实践智慧。

---

1. 亚里士多德:《尼各马可伦理学》,罗吉尔·克里斯普译,剑桥:剑桥大学出版社,2014 年,第 1 卷,第 1 章,1094a1—3。
2. 亚里士多德:《尼各马可伦理学》,第 7 卷,第 1 章,1145b2—7;参见克里斯托弗·希尔兹:"亚里士多德",选自《斯坦福哲学百科词典》(2015 秋季版),登录日期 2015 年 1 月 15 日,http://plato.stanford.edu/archives/fall2015/entries/aristotle/。
3. 亚里士多德:《尼各马可伦理学》,第 1 卷,第 4 章,1095a16—22。
4. 亚里士多德:《尼各马可伦理学》,第 1 卷,第 7 章,1098a16—18。

5. 亚里士多德:《尼各马可伦理学》,第 10 卷,第 9 章,1179b16—18 及第 2 卷,第 3 章,1104b12—13。
6. "公认观点"评估及方法评价,参见亚里士多德:《尼各马可伦理学》第 1 卷,第 4—5 页。
7. 亚里士多德:《尼各马可伦理学》,1172b28 及下页;柏拉图:《斐利布斯篇》,60c—61a。
8. 亚里士多德:《尼各马可伦理学》,第 2 卷,第 3 章,1104b3—11。
9. 亚里士多德:《尼各马可伦理学》,第 1 卷,第 6 章,1096b24;完整论述见第 1 章,第 6 节,1096b10—35。

4 作者贡献

要点

- 在《尼各马可伦理学》里，亚里士多德思考两个问题：幸福是不是人生活中最高的善？如果是，什么是获得幸福的必需条件？
- 亚里士多德认为德性是幸福的必要条件，但不是充分条件。幸福需要德性的行为，而不仅仅是灵魂的道德状态。
- 亚里士多德将哲学家柏拉图的伦理学理论和普通民众的观念结合起来，从中得出自己的观点。

作者目标

亚里士多德写作《尼各马可伦理学》的目的是寻找人生活中最高的善，[1] 以便向个人和政治家提供目标和行为模式。[2] 传统的智慧认为，幸福是每个人都追求的目标。在亚里士多德和其他古典派哲学家看来，幸福描述的是关于人的一系列客观事实，而不仅是关于人生的短暂的感觉和观点。有人认为在财富中可以找到幸福，有人在荣誉当中寻找幸福，也有人认为幸福在于权力，而亚里士多德哲学的领路人柏拉图和苏格拉底认为，幸福在于拥有美德。亚里士多德独创性的路径就是尝试融合这些看似矛盾的幸福的概念。

他的做法是强调人的善来自对于德性的实践，提出至善就是"灵魂合乎德性的行为"，以及"如果有多种德性，那么应该与最完整、最好的德性保持一致"。[3] 但是，拥有德性对于幸福只是必要条件，不是充分条件。要获得幸福，还必须拥有德性行为必需的外部条件（如友谊、经济资源等等）。没有这些外部条件，个体的道德品质就没有机会得以展现。例如，一个人想要展现慷慨的美德，却只拥有足够为自己购买食物和居所的财富，那他就无法体现这种美德。强调德性的行为，正是亚里士多德的独创。所以，认为亚里士多德强调好的品质而反对正确的行为是不正确的：他认为这两者都是幸福的必要条件。

上述内容阐明了亚里士多德的"德性伦理学"的一些内涵。（德性伦理学是亚里士多德提出的伦理学理论，认为判断一个行为是否道德应该依据个体的品质或者德性，而不是行为的结果。）

> "如果……我们认为人的典型活动是一种生活的方式，并且这种生活的方式是灵魂的活动和合乎理性的行为……而且当人的典型活动符合恰当的德性时，典型活动才能得以很好地完成，那么人的善就是灵魂合乎德性的行为。如果有多种德性，那么这种行为应该与最完整、最好的德性保持一致。"
>
> ——亚里士多德：《尼各马可伦理学》

研究方法

《尼各马可伦理学》中，亚里士多德对伦理学的研究方法是开创性的，主要体现在两个方面：一是他对实践的关注，二是他认为伦理反思需要伦理教育的观点。

亚里士多德发展了比他的老师柏拉图更加实际的伦理学方法。他认为，因为人的行为和社会充满了不可预见的事件和运气的成分，所以我们不能把伦理学当作抽象的学科。伦理学是实践性的。柏拉图使用了一个术语 *sophia* 来涵盖理论智慧和实践智慧，而亚里士多德将智慧划分为理论智慧（*sophia*）、实践智慧（*phronesis*）*

和创造智慧（创造事物的技巧）。所以，一个人不需要成为哲学家或者具备理论性的思维，也能拥有诸如正义、勇敢、节制等德性。[4]

此外，亚里士多德的伦理学方法既不同于他的领路人柏拉图的方法，也不同于大多数现代的伦理学路径，其主要差异在于他的研究并不是从伦理学概念的理论辩护切入。我们可以假设亚里士多德从以下两个问题入手：为什么幸福包含德性的活动？为什么传统的品质（如正义、节制、勇敢等）都可以成为德性？这样的阐述能够向每个人解释清楚我们为什么要正义、节制。事实上，柏拉图就是这样做的。在《理想国》中，他使用理性来解释美德（比如正义）。[5]

但是，亚里士多德为什么没有从这个问题入手呢？我们应该考虑到，在亚里士多德看来，一个人是否拥有关于什么是德性和什么不是德性的知识，在他发育的早期就被决定了。他曾多次指出，如果在一个人小时候，没有人教会他在追求欲望的同时要学会自律，他可能终身都与德性无缘。"任何人，"他说道，"想要在高尚和正义的领域学有所成……一定要接受良好的教养、形成好的习惯。"[6] 对于德性的理解可以稍后再来反思和提炼，但我们必须很早就掌握德性的本质，认识到德性是值得我们追求的最根本的目标。

时代贡献

《尼各马可伦理学》的主要思想是关于人的至善。一般认为，这种善是包涵幸福的，而且亚里士多德也承认，幸福是德性的、理性的活动。[7] 但是，亚里士多德也认可同时期雅典哲学关于幸福本质的辩论的价值。对于这些辩论，亚里士多德既有批判，又结合关于幸福的盛行观点作出了反馈。他批判了普通民众认为幸福就是拥有"快乐、财富、荣誉"的观点。[8] 在亚里士多德看来,追求这些事物,其实是在以它们的名义追求其他的事物。比如,人们追求金钱,其实是在追求金钱所能买到的事物。所以,它不能成为人类所有行为的根本目标。

此外,在德性品质是否是幸福的充分条件的问题上,亚里士多德和他的哲学前辈柏拉图和苏格拉底的意见相左。虽然拥有德性是必要条件,但如果一个有德之人,却是"丑陋的、出身低贱的,或者是鳏寡孤独",那他肯定无法获得幸福。[9] 可以推断,亚里士多德融合了传统幸福观念的精华部分。柏拉图和苏格拉底认为人需要德性品质才能幸福的观点是正确的,普通民众认为财富和荣誉使幸福成为可能的看法也是可取的。而亚里士多德认为,既具备道德德性又具备理智德性,同时还拥有德性行为必备的外在善的人,才是幸福之人。最后,亚里士多德赞同柏拉图的观点,认为哲学沉思的生活是人类所能达到的最高的善。

---

1. 亚里士多德:《尼各马可伦理学》,罗吉尔·克里斯普译,剑桥:剑桥大学出版社,2014 年,第 1 卷,第 2 章,1094a21—22 及第 4 章,1095a15—17。
2. 亚里士多德:《尼各马可伦理学》,第 1 卷,第 2 章,1094b11。
3. 亚里士多德:《尼各马可伦理学》,第 1 卷,第 7 章,1098a15—16。
4. 亚里士多德:《尼各马可伦理学》,第 6 卷,第 3—5 章,1139b14—1140b30。
5. 例子参见柏拉图:《理想国》,G. M. A. 格鲁布译,选自《古希腊哲学阅读》,马克·科恩、帕特丽夏·柯德和 C.D.C. 里夫编,印第安纳波利斯:哈克特出版社，2005 年，336b 及下页。
6. 亚里士多德:《尼各马可伦理学》，第 1 卷，第 4 章，1095b3—5。
7. 亚里士多德:《尼各马可伦理学》，第 1 卷，第 7 章，1098a16—17。
8. 亚里士多德:《尼各马可伦理学》，第 1 卷，第 4 章，1095a23—24。
9. 亚里士多德:《尼各马可伦理学》，第 1 卷，第 8 章，1099a31—1099b1—5。

第二部分：学术思想

5 思想主脉

要点

- 《尼各马可伦理学》的核心主题是幸福、德性和行为。要了解这些内容，需要详细地分析善的行为和品质、责任、正义、友谊和快乐等概念。
- 幸福是由德性的行为构成的；完全的德性需要道德德性（如勇敢）和理智德性，尤其是实践智慧。
- 亚里士多德认为实践智慧（希腊语：*phronesis*）帮助我们确定品质特征的两极之间的中道，而每一种德性代表了一种中道。

核心主题

亚里士多德《尼各马可伦理学》的根本目标是阐明人的至善。他认为德性行为是最高的善，他采用了五大概念来阐述他的观点：

- 幸福（希腊语：*eudaimonia*）
- 人类的功能（希腊语：*ergon*）
- 德性（希腊语：*aretê*）
- 实践智慧（希腊语：*phronesis*）
- 中道思想

在第 1 卷第 7 章，我们可以得知最重要的善是幸福。这是一个"有声望的观点"（又译"公认观点"或"共同意见"，*endoxa*），是一整套条理清晰的道德哲学得以建立的出发点。

但是，亚里士多德是如何理解"幸福"的呢？它不仅仅是一种主观的情感状态——就像我们今天所认为的，可以通过感觉来自行定义的事物；它更是一种客观的状态，近似于健康和繁荣的概念。而幸福，或者叫做繁荣，是由功能*（定义一个事物的"典型行为"，希腊语 ergon）决定的。

更进一步讲，所有人类共有的典型行为就是按照某种思维和行动的德性（aretê）来生活。[1] 思维的德性就是"理智德性"，而行为的德性被称作"道德德性"。最后，每一种德性都是至少两个互相对应的恶习之间的中道。

> "亚里士多德的《尼各马可伦理学》讨论了'对人类来说，什么是善'。它提出并回答了一个问题，'什么是人最主要的善？'同时，它也着眼于这个答案的内涵。"
> ——莎拉·布罗迪：《〈尼各马可伦理学〉哲学指南》

思想探究

《尼各马可伦理学》的目标是阐明人的至善。为了阐明什么是幸福，亚里士多德追问"什么是人的功能（即典型行为，希腊语 ergon）"。亚里士多德认为，理性是把人和石头、植物以及其他动物区分开来的特征，所以对幸福的阐述必须建立在人是理性动物这一事实的基础上。他指出，人的功能（也就是人的幸福之匙）是依照德性（aretê）行事，因为德性行为是与人的理性本质一致的。

人的理性本质是实践智慧和理论智慧的结合。实践智慧（phronesis）是亚里士多德的理论体系中非常重要的理智德性，因为它使德性生活成为可能。亚里士多德写道，"一个人拥有实践智慧的标志就是能够考虑清楚什么是对他本人来讲是善的、该做的事情。"² 具有实践智慧的人从两个方面来做到这一点。首先，他要能够判断特定情形下什么是道德的事情（以及如何去做这件事情）。其次，实践智慧帮助有德性的人控制他的欲望，否则他会与合乎道德德性的行为背道而驰。正如亚里士多德所强调的那样，通过实践智慧对行为的判断和对欲望的节制，涉及到在特定环境当中恰当的"感觉和行动"。³

有人可能会问，为什么实践智慧要求依据德性行事？亚里士多德认为实践智慧能帮助我们确定哪些品质特征体现了品质的两极之间的中道。例如，实践智慧会告诉我们，勇敢是鲁莽和懦弱这两个极端品质的中道。鲁莽就是闯入不必要的危险环境，或者是缺乏恰当的计划；懦弱是在危险的情形面前退缩——即便需要采取行动来帮助他人。所以，这两者之间的中道——勇敢——就是即便面对人身伤害的危险也要去完成善举的决心。此外，实践智慧能帮助我们认识到，尽管在人生的每一个领域都只能有一个值得追求的德性，但需要避免的对应的恶习却可能有很多个。

那么，亚里士多德认为哪些德性和幸福相关呢？德性是关于思维和行为的根深蒂固的品质特征，包括道德德性（如正义、节制、慷慨、友谊、勇敢等）和理智德性（如才智、科学知识（或其他某种知识）、实践智慧等）。这些德性仅仅依靠教育是无法获得的，只能通过长期的、道德的习惯才能养成。

最后，理论理性是另一个区分人和动物的特征。一个完全幸福的人生中，人能够沉思抽象的、普遍的真理。人和动物的另一个区分，就是人具有哲学地生活的可能性。也正是这一点，使人更接近于神。⁴ 因此，对亚里士多德而言，幸福生活是这样发展的：

- 从幼年时期开始，接受良好的教育，养成正确的习惯；
- 通过实践这些习惯，最终发展理智德性和道德德性；
- 理智德性和道德德性的结合使人具备实践上的智慧——能够认识道德的行为，并且为了德性，始终如一地选择道德的行为；
- 最终，一个幸福的人能够拥有德性行为和思考抽象的哲学问题必备的资源。一个过着由符合道德德性和理智德性的行为构成的生活的人，是真正幸福的人。

语言表述

众所周知，《尼各马可伦理学》的文字高度浓缩，这很可能是因为它是用来给吕克昂学园的专业人才讲授的系列课程。所以，亚里士多德这部著作的最初的听众，是受过良好的哲学教育和道德教育的人。而且，亚里士多德讲课时，很有可能使用了插图甚至是直观教具的方法，来详细阐述他的要点。

《尼各马可伦理学》的语言对其后的道德哲学家们产生了重大的影响。有三个词汇影响非常深远。首先，亚里士多德对希腊词汇 *eudaimonia*（幸福）的使用，引发了一种特殊的关于伦理学*的思考方法。"幸福"伦理学的理论围绕丰富的幸福观展开，并以其作为伦理学的目的。亚里士多德创造的另一个重要的概念是实践智慧，也叫实践理性（*phronesis*）。之后的大多数伦理学理论都尝试阐述理论理性和实践理性之间的关系。最后，亚里士多德坚持认为人类的行为是有某种目的（*telos*）的。这个词催生了目的论*伦理学。目的论伦理学通常专注于发现或描述所有人类行为所指向（或应该指向）的目标。

1. 亚里士多德:《尼各马可伦理学》,罗吉尔·克里斯普译,剑桥:剑桥大学出版社,2014年,第1卷,第13章,1103a1—10。
2. 亚里士多德:《尼各马可伦理学》,第6卷,第5章,1140a25。
3. 亚里士多德:《尼各马可伦理学》,第2卷,第6章,1106b17。
4. 亚里士多德:《尼各马可伦理学》,第10卷,7—8。

6 思想支脉

要点

- 对于为什么人们无法做到明知是正确的事情,亚里士多德给出了新的解释。
- 正义和友谊,这两大与我们社会生活直接相关的德性,对于真正的幸福和繁荣是必不可少的。
- 亚里士多德虽然承认善的快乐是善的生活的关键,但他也指出快乐不是至善。

其他思想

亚里士多德《尼各马可伦理学》中,有分量的其他思想有自发行为与责任、快乐与痛苦、意志薄弱*、正义与友谊,以及总体的德性的人生等。

亚里士多德发现,责备和赞扬只对于那些能够控制自己行为的人才有意义。有人可能会说,缺乏德性的人是因为沉溺于不道德的习惯、无法选择德性的行为。亚里士多德这样回应:缺乏德性的人应该为自己选择背离德性品质、趋附邪恶品质的行为负责。

亚里士多德也认为享乐对人的行为非常重要:"道德德性与享乐和痛苦有关;正是为了享乐,我们才会做坏事;正是因为痛苦,我们才摒弃了善行。"[1] 享乐会使我们做出不好的行为,缺乏自我控制,因此享乐通常不是善。但是,当享乐与德性的行为联系在一起时,它就是善。例如,如果一个道德的人认为他需要作出勇敢的自我牺牲,那么对他来说,这个行为就是享乐。

> "（亚里士多德的）一些观点是如此精彩，如此令人信服，我们感到可惜的是没有诺贝尔哲学奖（可以颁发给他）……这些绝妙的思维当中，有一项是我们时至今日仍应心怀感激的，那就是他在伦理学思考中，创造性地把享乐和痛苦综合起来的方法。"
>
> ——多罗西娅·弗雷德*:《亚里士多德伦理学中的享乐与痛苦》

思想探究

亚里士多德阐述享乐与痛苦时，也讨论了与之相关的意志薄弱（*akrasia*）的问题。这个问题就是，既然幸福（*eudaimonia*）是作为人的所有行动的目标的德性行为，为什么人们不能做到道德的行动呢？甚至是那些明知什么才能带来幸福的人也无法做到呢？柏拉图曾经指出，如果人们不依照美德来行事，他们肯定是出于无知。他认为，一个人不可能明知拿走他人的财物是不正义的，还依然选择这样的行为。而亚里士多德试图解释一个明显的事实——人们经常无法做到明知是正确的事情。他的观点是，出现这样的问题，是因为这些人"意志薄弱"——他用这个术语来描述缺乏自我约束的人。他认为，意志薄弱就像是永远地陷入了一种"昏睡、疯狂或者沉醉"的状态。[2]

举个现代的例子，醉酒的人可能声称自己知道酒后驾车是错误的，但如果他还是酒后驾车了，我们也不会感到惊奇。虽然醉酒的人和清醒的人使用着相同的词汇，当他们喃喃自语"酒后驾车是不对的"的时候，他们并不真正了解自己话语的含义。因此，不能说他们真正地知道什么是错误的行为。

与此类似的是，意志薄弱的人（即缺乏自我约束的人）受到自身欲望的影响，不能真正理解他认为正确的道德要求。要克服意志薄弱，人要接受教育，学会习惯性地选择道德的行为。一旦建立起选择道德行为的能力（并且因为该行为是道德的而去执行），人就不再是意志薄弱的，而是道德的。

要更好地理解亚里士多德的幸福观，一定要理解他的德性不是极度个人主义的，不是向内心寻求的。亚里士多德认为道德哲学的任务是和政治关切一脉相承的。所以，正义和友谊是亚里士多德伦理体系中重要的善，因为幸福繁荣的人生一定包涵这些要素。在《尼各马可伦理学》第5卷，亚里士多德探讨了正义这一德性，而在第8卷和第9卷，他探讨了友谊的善。他发现了正义的两个层面——一个可以叫作政治正义，另一个叫作个人正义。政治正义是在拥有极大财富的人和没有财富的人之间，追求一种中道的状态。[3] 正义的个人层面是给予人们应该得到的事物的个人德性，它是相对应的恶习之间的中道。非法的、贪婪的、不公正的人错失中道，因而是不正义的。[4]

亚里士多德认为，友谊有三种类型：出于利益（便利）的友谊、出于享乐的友谊、出于德性的友谊。[5] 前两者最为常见，有时也是友谊的必要形式；而第三种友谊是真挚、持久的："完满的友谊是善人的友谊，是德性相近的人之间的友谊。"[6] 亚里士多德对正义和友谊的阐述中非常有趣的一点，是他在《尼各马可伦理学》和《政治学》中提出，城邦（希腊语：*polis*）应该在发展民众的品质方面发挥作用，以使民众拥有正义的德性。

最后，亚里士多德对德性的理解是幸福只适用于对总体的生活而言。他认为，一个人不可能因为仅仅某一个行为就变得有道德。相反的是，道德的人只有在生命结束的时候才能加以判断，而他会终身拥有德性的行为，这能使他获得幸福。亚里士多德说，德性是真正的存在于"完全的人生中的，因为一燕不成夏，一天也同样成就不了夏天"。[7] 换言之，一个人做过一次公平交易，并不能说明他一定是正义的。

被忽视之处

《尼各马可伦理学》是历史上被研究最多的哲学文本之一，但也有一些被忽略的方面。其中一个被一定程度上忽略的地方，是亚里士多德认为具有豪迈*德性的人（即展示出适当的骄傲和宽容大量的人）是德性的最高楷模。一个豪迈的人对自己的慷慨大度引以为豪，相信自己应当获得宏大的荣耀，并且十分清楚自己相对于他人的道德优越性。亚里士多德把这样的豪迈看做是一种"类似于德性的王冠"的品质。[8] 尽管这种把豪迈当作德性成就的观念和现代的道德观念并不一致，但它却是《尼各马可伦理学》非常重要的一个方面。

另一个在很大程度上被忽略的方面，是亚里士多德的道德体系中与沉思的人生（即对于永恒真理的反思）以及沉思与神的关系相关观点。在《尼各马可伦理学》第10卷，亚里士多德回到了最高的善的问题。他提出，尽管遵照德性行事能获得幸福的生活，但是还有更加完满的事情：哲学反思的人生。"如果幸福是合乎德性的活动，"他说，"那它应该合乎最高的德性……这种活动是沉思性的。"[9]

亚里士多德的人的概念，是建立在"我们从本质上来说都是理性的"这样一个认识之上的。因此，对数学、形而上学*的真理（关于最终存在的真理）以及关于上帝的真理进行沉思的人，[10] 能够获得最高的幸福，也最近似于上帝。

1. 亚里士多德:《尼各马可伦理学》,罗吉尔·克里斯普译,剑桥:剑桥大学出版社,2014年,第2卷,第3章,1104b9—10。
2. 亚里士多德:《尼各马可伦理学》,第7卷,第3章,1147a14。
3. 亚里士多德:《尼各马可伦理学》,1133b32。
4. 亚里士多德:《尼各马可伦理学》,第5卷,第1章,1129a32。
5. 亚里士多德:《尼各马可伦理学》,第8卷,第3章,1156a6—1156b35。
6. 亚里士多德:《尼各马可伦理学》,第8卷,第3章,1156b8。
7. 亚里士多德:《尼各马可伦理学》,第1卷,第7章,1098a16—17。
8. 亚里士多德:《尼各马可伦理学》,第4卷,第3章,1124a2。
9. 约翰·库珀:"沉思与幸福:重新思考",选自《理性与情感:古代道德哲学与伦理学理论选读》,新泽西普林斯顿:普林斯顿大学出版社,1999年,第212—236页。
10. 亚里士多德:《欧德谟伦理学》,布莱德·英伍德、拉斐尔·沃尔夫编,剑桥:剑桥大学出版社,2013年,1249b15—25。

7 历史成就

要点 🗝

- 亚里士多德提供了一个完整清晰的、以人的幸福为核心的伦理生活的体系。
- 亚里士多德关于人的本质的概念是他发展德性理论的关键,而德性又是幸福的核心。
- 亚里士多德确定的具体德性源于对人的本质的思考,但这些德性也受到文化的影响。

观点评价

《尼各马可伦理学》的核心目标是定义好的生活。在这个过程中,他阐明了幸福、德性、实践智慧、快乐、友谊等概念。他进行了复杂而又详细的人类学*(此处指关于人的本质的一系列观念)研究,促成了这一不朽之作。相较于同时期其他形式的道德哲学*,《尼各马可伦理学》之所以脱颖而出,一方面是因为它系统、完整的结构框架,另一方面是因为它尝试从一个视角来阐述人的多种激情和欲望。亚里士多德用极具说服力的论证,反驳了把幸福等同于财富、声望和权利的思想。与此相似的是,他也指出德性品质本身并不等同于幸福,因为具备道德却遭受痛苦折磨的人生活也不那么幸福。幸福之人,不但拥有德性,还应具备一些外部善——比如友谊和快乐。

亚里士多德也改进了柏拉图认为一个人之所以选择做错误的事情是因为缺乏知识的观点。他使用了"意志薄弱"这个概念,指出尽管人们拥有关于什么是正确的事情的知识,他们还有可能会犯错,因为他们的欲望和激情没有受过训练。但是,亚里士多德对于德性活动的强调提出了这样一个问题:如果要在自己的行动中模仿德性的品质,我们首先应该如何确定哪些人是道德的呢(可以做我们模仿的榜样)?

一些哲学家曾经指出,有道德的人自然能够向我们展示哪些是正确的行为。但在亚里士多德看来,如果说我们知道哪些人是道德的,是因为他们会做出正确的行动,那是一个死循环(逻辑推理的谬误)。

> "亚里士多德目前在道德哲学领域占据了特权地位……(他)的伦理学的哲学研究的方法,是该学科的所有学生都应该学习(但并不一定接受)的。胜过任何其他古代的哲学家的是……他的作品仍被研读,他伦理学的框架仍然可行。"
> ——理查德·克劳特:《布莱克维尔〈尼各马可伦理学〉指南》

当时的成就

想要确定像《尼各马可伦理学》这样古老的著作的直接影响是非常困难的,一部分原因是,从公元前323年到公元前45年,在亚里士多德自己的哲学流派之外,几乎没有任何对于这部著作的引用。[1] 公元前1世纪,斯多葛学派*和伊壁鸠鲁学派*的伦理学非常流行,而亚里士多德的伦理学观点似乎变得黯然失色。斯多葛学派的追随者们坚持由哲学家苏格拉底提出的著名观点,即美德是幸福的充分条件,而不是像亚里士多德所认为的仅仅是一个必要条件。另一方面,伊壁鸠鲁学派的追随者们将幸福等同于享乐。但是,值得注意的是,学界一般认为,《尼各马可伦理学》对斯多葛学派和伊壁鸠鲁学派的伦理学都产生了重大的影响。[2]

社会和政治因素对《尼各马可伦理学》的接受起到了重大的作用。例如,在亚里士多德于公元前 322 年去世之前,他指定自己的追随者泰奥弗拉斯托斯*为继任者。一些古代文本中提及,当泰奥弗拉斯托斯于公元前 287 年去世时,根据他的遗嘱中的一项条款,亚里士多德的著作被从吕克昂学园的学生手中拿走。[3] 他的《尼各马可伦理学》和其他学术著作,直到公元前 86 年罗马占领雅典的时候才得以恢复。他的一些其他作品,12 世纪之前在欧洲根本无法找到。

《尼各马可伦理学》于中世纪晚期(约 12 世纪至 15 世纪)一经重新出现,立刻对伦理学发展的前景产生了关键的影响。例如,在 13 世纪,中世纪基督教思想的重要学者托马斯·阿奎那*尝试将亚里士多德伦理学和基督教圣经的教义结合起来。阿奎那整合了亚里士多德对审慎、勇敢、正义、实践智慧等德性的作用的阐述。他还重申了沉思生活的至高地位,指出亚里士多德鼓励人追求沉思上帝的生活。[4]

局限性

《尼各马可伦理学》的三个哲学点导致了它被接受过程中的局限,这三个点是:

- 亚里士多德关于人类的功能(ergon)的观点
- 他确定德性的方法
- 他提出的受文化影响的德目

首先，以上三者中最重要的一个，是亚里士多德关于人的客观功能（*ergon*）*的概念。这个概念指的是所有人都有的功能或者目的——即便人们并不知道它的存在。从人的本质中可以发现一个客观的功能，因此可以提供人的幸福之匙，这是亚里士多德的伦理学体系建立的基础概念。而这个功能，就是合乎理性的德性行为。

"人类拥有天生的功能"这一思想在亚里士多德时代的雅典可能很容易被接受，但是具有更现代、更科学的世界观的人往往会排斥它。事实上，在反对亚里士多德伦理学的意见中，有一项也同样用以反对他的科学思想。亚里士多德曾经说过事物从本质上来说既具有目的性的（根本性的）原因*，又具有物理性原因。也就是说，他认为不光可以了解自然界一个变化的物理原因（客观原因），还可以了解引起这一变化的自然界的目的。但是，由于17世纪的科学革命将科学限制在对于客观原因的探究中，因此，亚里士多德关于生物的功能和人的功能的观点，常常被认为是不科学的。

其次，很多哲学家质疑，亚里士多德的理论如何能够帮助个人判断在特定情境下应该如何行事。亚里士多德认为实践智慧（*phronesis*）能够帮助我们判断一个行为是正义的或不正义的、勇敢的或是怯懦的。但是，一个人只有拥有很高程度的德性的时候，才能够拥有实践智慧。问题在于，在一个人知道应该发展哪些德性之前，他应该首先已经具备这些德性。有一些哲学家认为，这是一个有缺陷的循环论证。[5]

最后，尽管亚里士多德的德目是面向所有人类的，但是他的阐述却局限在他对人的本质的个别理解之上[6]——而在今天，大家普遍认为不同的文化的德性观是具有根本性差异的。[7]

虽然亚里士多德宣称他列出了所有的德性，[8]但是他的德目中没有包含一些后世所看重的德性。例如，它并没有包括基督教的重要德性，如贞洁和谦逊；它也没有包括现代有环保意识这样的德性。[9]所以，亚里士多德《尼各马可伦理学》中的一些伦理概念，可能只适用于特定时期和特定人群。

---

1. 凯伦·M. 尼尔森："希腊时期哲学中的《尼各马可伦理学》——隐藏的宝藏？"，选自《亚里士多德伦理学的接受》，剑桥：剑桥大学出版社，2012年，第5页。
2. 凯伦·M. 尼尔森："希腊时期哲学中的《尼各马可伦理学》"，第5—7页，第19—30页。
3. 凯伦·M. 尼尔森："希腊时期哲学中的《尼各马可伦理学》"，第12页。
4. 拉尔夫·麦金纳里和奥卡拉汉·约翰："圣托马斯·阿奎那"，选自《斯坦福哲学百科词典》（2014年5月23日），登录日期2015年12月10日，http://plato.stanford.edu/archives/aquinas/ #ThoAri。
5. 麦凯：《伦理学：发明对与错》，伦敦：企鹅出版社，1977年，第186页。
6. 亚里士多德：《尼各马可伦理学》，大卫·罗斯译，选自《亚里士多德全集》，普林斯顿：普林斯顿大学出版社，1991年，第1卷，第7章，1097b22—1098a20。
7. 关于品质的德性（即我们所谓的"道德德性"）的讨论，参见亚里士多德：《尼各马可伦理学》，第3卷，第6章—第5卷，第11章。
8. 亚里士多德：《尼各马可伦理学》，第3卷，第6章，1115a5及第4卷，第7章，1127a16—17。
9. 罗莎琳德·赫斯特豪斯："美德伦理学"，选自《斯坦福哲学百科词典》（2013秋季版），登录日期2016年2月27日，http://plato.stanford.edu/archives/fall2013/entries/ethics-virtue/。

8 著作地位

要点 🔑

- 亚里士多德的哲学作品涵盖了他所在的时代几乎所有的领域（如自然科学、心理学、数学、修辞学*、政治学）。他甚至还发明了新的科学学科，如逻辑学和生物学。
- 《尼各马可伦理学》基于他早期讲授的伦理学课程，是一部以亚里士多德其他作品为基础的集大成之作。
- 《尼各马可伦理学》是广泛研究的产物，是亚里士多德最伟大的作品之一。它会一直是亚里士多德全集*的精华所在。

定位

《尼各马可伦理学》最有可能创作于亚里士多德最多产的时期，也就是公元前335年到公元前323年，他第二次在雅典生活的时期。他的大多数作品都是创作于这个时期。大多数流传至今的作品都是粗略写成的课堂讲稿，或者是他的吕克昂学园的讨论会的论文。《尼各马可伦理学》并不是唯一一本署名亚里士多德的伦理学专著。早些时候他还写作了《欧德谟伦理学》（很可能是以他的学生的名字命名的）。《大伦理学》也被认为是亚里士多德创作的，但大多数学者都认为尽管该书包涵了亚里士多德学派的主要观点，却并不是亚里士多德亲自写作的。[1]

《尼各马可伦理学》和《欧德谟伦理学》之间的关系很难确定——两本著作中有三分之一的内容是相同的，这更增加了这个问题的难度。一位美国现代亚里士多德研究者克里斯·波波尼奇*说：

"更为常见的学术观点是认为《尼各马可伦理学》创作得稍晚一些，它至少是从公元前1世纪或2世纪开始，就被认为是亚里士多德主要的代表性作品。"[2] 大多数诠释者都认为《尼各马可伦理学》比《欧德谟伦理学》更重要，而且学者们把它看做亚里士多德道德思想的顶峰。这一点可以由它几乎吸收了亚里士多德哲学所有其他部分的精华这一事实得到证明。这些部分的内容包括逻辑学、关于人的灵魂的思想、形而上学（研究存在和实体本质等基础问题的哲学分支），以及他的政治哲学等。《政治学》是从《尼各马可伦理学》结尾的第10卷开端的。两部著作可以看作一个统一的整体。

> "亚里士多德文集中含有两部冠以'伦理学'之名的著述：《尼各马可伦理学》与《欧德谟伦理学》……《尼各马可伦理学》可能是亚里士多德暮年执掌吕克昂学园时（即他五六十岁时）完成的。"
>
> ——大卫·罗斯：《亚里士多德〈尼各马可伦理学〉》

整合

亚里士多德的作品数量相当惊人：古代记录记载他创作了150多本著作[3]，其中有很多——尤其是流传甚广的对话——都遗失了，以英语译本算仅有大约2450页保留了下来。现在的亚里士多德文集是由罗得岛的安德罗尼柯*编辑的——他可能是公元前1世纪吕克昂学园的领袖。安德罗尼柯首创了著名的哲学词汇"形而上学"（字面意思为"物理学之后"）。他以此为亚里士多德的著作命名，是由于将其排列在关于物理学的著作之后。现存的文本给人一种未完结的感觉，这使得学者们认为，这些文本或者是亚里士多德多次修订和重写的课堂讲稿，或者是他的某位学生的课堂笔记。

从古代起，亚里士多德的文集被划分为界限分明的五大领域，划分的依据不是创作的时间，而是作品的内容。这五大领域为：

- 逻辑学著作《工具论》（希腊语：*Organon*，即"工具"），一部影响深远的文集，在中世纪被用来教授逻辑和辩论
- 关于自然和生物学的里程碑式的著作
- 《形而上学》，探究实体的终极本质
- 对人的行为的研究，包括两部伦理学专著*——《尼各马可伦理学》和《欧德谟伦理学》以及《政治学》
- 一部关于悲剧理论的著作和著名的《修辞学》[4]

亚里士多德的伦理学、政治学作品与其他作品之间最重要的关联，或许是它们与生物学理论之间的关系。尽管亚里士多德花了大量的时间详细描述和划分物种，但他似乎也认为生物物种有特定的功能和目的——类似于他对人的本质的理解。在他看来，有一些特定的功能把人和其他动物区分开来，因此能向我们提供人行事和生活的智慧。

意义

《尼各马可伦理学》和亚里士多德的全部著作的重要作用，再怎么夸大都不为过。美国一位教授罗恩·波兰斯基*写道："亚里士多德的《尼各马可伦理学》是第一批系统性地研究伦理学的著作之一，而且可能是有史以来这一领域最为重要、最具影响力的哲学著作。亚里士多德继承了苏格拉底和柏拉图思想的荣光，对所有重大的探究领域都有了深入的了解，他的目标是创作一部能够经得住时间考验的、综合性的伦理学著述。"[5]

众多紧密追随他的哲学思想的人，被称作亚里士多德学派，也叫逍遥学派 Peripatetics，得名于吕克昂学园旁边的圆形廊道（希腊语：*peripatos*）。

中世纪晚期（约公元 1200—1500 年），亚里士多德哲学的影响力极度强大。在此期间，亚里士多德被称为"唯一的哲学家"，大都认为他的作品代表了关于世界的最高智慧。一些伟大的思想家，如意大利天文学家伽利略*、法国哲学家笛卡尔*、波兰天文学家哥白尼*等，于 16、17 世纪开始脱离亚里士多德关于自然的理论，尤其是在物理学和天文学领域。此外，道德哲学家——如休谟*和康德*——于 18 世纪脱离他的思想。但是，尽管历经这些历史变化，《尼各马可伦理学》在道德哲学领域一直保持了最为重要的经典著作的地位。

关于亚里士多德的文献数量众多——尤其是研究《尼各马可伦理学》的。《尼各马可伦理学》在当代道德哲学中也发挥了重大的作用。最近的以道德品质为伦理核心的"德性伦理学"运动，就是受到了亚里士多德强调道德行为中德性观点的启发。现代著名的道德哲学家，如英国德性伦理学家费丽帕·福特*、苏格兰思想家阿拉斯代尔·麦金泰尔*、美国学者玛莎·努斯鲍姆*等，都是亚里士多德思想的追随者。[6]

---

1. 支持《大伦理学》真实性的观点参见约翰·库伯："《大伦理学》与亚里士多德道德哲学"，《美国语言学杂志》，1973 年，第 327—349 页。反对意见参见

罗·克里斯托弗:"对约翰·库伯关于《大伦理学》看法的回应",《美国语言学杂志》,1975年,第160—172页。

2. 参见亚里士多德:《尼各马可伦理学》,大卫·罗斯译,选自《亚里士多德全集》,普林斯顿:普林斯顿大学出版社,1991年,viii;以及克里斯·波波尼奇:"亚里士多德伦理学著作",选自《布莱克维尔〈尼各马可伦理学〉指南》,理查德·克劳特编,第12—36页,牛津:威利—布莱克维尔出版社,2006年。对标准观点最尖锐的批评来自安东尼·肯尼:《亚里士多德伦理学:〈欧德谟伦理学〉与〈尼各马可伦理学〉关系研究》,牛津:克拉伦登出版社,1978年。

3. 第欧根尼·拉尔修:《名哲言行录》,R.D.希克斯编,马萨诸塞州坎布里奇:哈佛大学出版社,1966年。

4. 以上著作均参见巴恩斯:《亚里士多德全集》。

5. 罗纳德·波兰斯基:"导读:作为实践科学的伦理学",选自《剑桥〈尼各马可伦理学〉指南》,罗纳德·波兰斯基编,剑桥:剑桥大学出版社,2014年。

6. 玛莎·努斯鲍姆:"不相关的美德:亚里士多德主义路径",选自《生活质量》,玛莎·努斯鲍姆和阿马蒂亚·森编,第242—69页,牛津:克拉伦登出版社,1993年。

第三部分：学术影响

9 最初反响

要点

- 《尼各马可伦理学》很可能是亚里士多德更早的一部作品《欧德谟伦理学》的修订本。
- 建立一个完整的、自书成之日起的《尼各马可伦理学》批评史是不可能的。
- 《尼各马可伦理学》出版后的几个世纪中,与之争锋的道德体系有斯多葛学派、伊壁鸠鲁学派、怀疑主义学派*等亚里士多德同时期的其他思想家建立的道德行为的研究路径。

批评

对于《尼各马可伦理学》的直接影响,无论是正面的还是负面的评价都不容易得出。不同于柏拉图关于政府的重要著作《理想国》——该书引发了不少古希腊和古罗马读者的回应——《尼各马可伦理学》似乎根本未曾出版过。从现存的文本来看,在公元前1世纪西塞罗(公元前106—43年)的《论目的》(又译《论至善与至恶》)之前,没有任何对于《尼各马可伦理学》的引用。这说明在亚里士多德生前,或者在他于公元前322年去世之后的一个时期内,《尼各马可伦理学》可能没有在吕克昂学园之外流通过。这也解释了为什么该书没有受到直接批评,亚里士多德也没有对批评意见做出任何回应。

但是,亚里士多德的哲学立场因该书而众所周知,而所有希腊时期*(得名于希腊语 *Hellas*(意为希腊),从公元前323年亚历山大大帝去世至公元前 31 年罗马帝国建立）影响重大的学派，如斯多葛学派、伊壁鸠鲁学派、怀疑主义学派等，都可能对其进行过思考（即便没有《尼各马可伦理学》这个名字，至少他们也思考过它的思想精神）。斯多葛学派不接受亚里士多德认为外部善是幸福必备条件的观点，他们持有苏格拉底的观点，认为美德足以使人获得幸福。伊壁鸠鲁学派将幸福等同于适度的享乐，而不是理性灵魂的活动。怀疑主义学派不赞同亚里士多德认为我们能够认识德性的观点，他们宣称哲学的反思并不能帮助我们发现或者获得德性。

> "完成《尼各马可伦理学》在希腊哲学中的接受史，是一件几乎不可能的任务。问题不是缺乏证据那么简单。我们找不到任何的援引，可以把伊壁鸠鲁学派、斯多葛学派或者学院派哲学家（即源自柏拉图学园的对伦理学知识持怀疑主义态度的信徒）所探讨的教义，与《尼各马可伦理学》中亚里士多德明确辩护的观点联系起来。"
> ——凯伦·M. 尼尔森："希腊时期哲学中的《尼各马可伦理学》"

回应

对于道德哲学史，特伦斯·欧文教授曾经说过，"我们可以通过一条重要的线把道德哲学的历史贯穿起来，那就是去思考亚里士多德在多大程度上是正确的，以及他的继承者们对他观点的看法。"[1] 但从《尼各马可伦理学》的最初反应来看，其影响很难评估，因为关于亚里士多德生前人们对《尼各马可伦理学》的回应，我们几乎没有直接证据。

但是，我们确实知道，在后来的古代时期，确实存在亚里士多德伦理学体系的拥护者。例如，生活在2世纪晚期和3世纪早期的阿佛洛狄西亚的亚历山大*，反对斯多葛学派认为完美地践行美德是人的全部目标的观点。他认为，有道德的人也希望自己的行为能够达成其目的。而斯多葛学派则认为，一个人捐出的善款是否最终到达需要它们的人的手中并不重要：如果一个人做出了道德的行为，且善款被误用也不是出于他自身的失误，那么他的行为就是最高的善。阿佛洛狄西亚的亚历山大为他所理解的亚里士多德的观点进行辩护：亚里士多德强调，达成目的对于道德上的善行是非常重要的。[2] 因此，亚里士多德并没有亲自与他的批评者们论战过，他的思想的拥护者们替他进行了辩护。这是亚里士多德学派哲学史上多次出现，也将会继续出现的一个模式。

冲突与共识

我们没有直接的历史证据证明亚里士多德的伦理学观点曾经受到批评，或者他因此而修订了自己的观点。这主要是亚里士多德和今天的读者之间的历史距离造成的。认为亚里士多德没有考虑过当时的批评——或者没有出现任何围绕他的伦理思想的批判性的交流和互动——绝对是错误的看法。恰恰相反，因为亚里士多德曾在柏拉图学园求学，又曾是吕克昂学园的领袖，所以在他的哲学生涯中，很可能接受过关于他的思想的反馈和批评。

此外，大多数学者认为亚里士多德是《尼各马可伦理学》和《欧德谟伦理学》这两部伦理学著作的作者。[3] 但是，很重要的一点是，尽管这两部著述中有三卷书的内容是相同的（即《尼各马可伦理学》第5—7卷和《欧德谟伦理学》第4—6卷），但是这两者包涵的重要伦理学概念是有差异的。例如，两部著作中实践智慧

（*phronesis*）的概念并不一致。在《欧德谟伦理学》里，实践智慧是一个抽象的理论概念（类似于柏拉图的术语"智慧"——*sophia*＊），而在《尼各马可伦理学》中，它完全是实践性的。[4] 因为亚里士多德的最终观点是把科学划分为理论活动、实践活动和生产活动，所以很有可能的是亚里士多德先写了《欧德谟伦理学》，在修正了某些伦理概念后再写了《尼各马可伦理学》。这一解释和亚里士多德逐渐脱离柏拉图的哲学立场的事实也是一致的。不过，这个解释是建立在文本自身本质的基础上的，缺乏外部的证据。

---

1. 特伦斯·欧文：《伦理学发展史》，第1卷，牛津：牛津大学出版社，2007年，第4页。
2. 亚里士多德：《尼各马可伦理学》，罗吉尔·克里斯普译，剑桥：剑桥大学出版社，2014年，第10卷，第7章，1177b16—26。
3. 罗吉尔·克里斯普："导读"，选自《尼各马可伦理学》，vii—viii。
4. 弗雷德里克·科普勒斯顿：《科普勒斯顿哲学史：希腊与罗马》. 伦敦：康蒂纽姆出版社，2003年，第270页。

10 后续争议

要点

- 亚里士多德对德性的系统探讨极大地影响了基督教和非基督教的德性观。
- 亚里士多德去世后，他的哲学——包括伦理学——由他的追随者（即逍遥学派）继承下来，而柏拉图*思想的拥护者则对此进行了批判性的继承。
- 中世纪基督教学者托马斯·阿奎那对亚里士多德伦理学进行了解读，他把人的本质看做德性和善行的关键。新亚里士多德学派*——亚里士多德观点的继承者——又继续探讨托马斯·阿奎那的这一解读。

应用与问题

尽管创作于公元前 335 年至公元前 323 年之间的《尼各马可伦理学》是哲学史上最具影响力的著作之一，但在不同的时期，它的受欢迎程度和影响力不尽相同。亚里士多德逝世后的一段时期内，他的伦理学的发展主要是在他的吕克昂学园之内。这一学派的成员被称作逍遥学派。在希腊时期（公元前 322 年至公元前 31 年）和罗马时期*（公元前 27 年至公元 395 年），他的伦理学体系被斯多葛学派和伊壁鸠鲁学派伦理学光芒掩盖——后两者对于幸福生活给出了不同的定义。

伊壁鸠鲁学派是希腊哲学家伊壁鸠鲁（公元前 341 年至公元前 270 年）创建的，他认为幸福是由享乐*（希腊语：*hedone*）构成的。伊壁鸠鲁把快乐定义为"身体的无痛苦和灵魂的无纷扰",他认为美德(如正义和节制等)可以保护人,使其免于遭受由于无差别地追求快乐而带来的心理痛苦[1]——这一观点和亚里士多德的观点是矛盾的。在亚里士多德看来,德性行为就是幸福,而享乐是与幸福一致的;而伊壁鸠鲁则认为享乐就是幸福,美德是获得享乐的方法。虽然没有直接证据表明亚里士多德伦理学对伊壁鸠鲁学派伦理学有影响,但一些学者认为两者的核心范畴相同,因此这种影响是存在的。[2]

斯多葛学派继承了苏格拉底和柏拉图的思想,认为德性品质是幸福的充足条件。虽然这一观点和亚里士多德的幸福观互相矛盾,但很多学者认为亚里士多德对斯多葛学派的伦理概念产生了影响。一个例子就是斯多葛学派强调"合乎本性"的行为——这和亚里士多德强调通过研究人的本质来确定伦理的观点是相似的。[3] 因此,从某种意义上讲,伊壁鸠鲁学派和斯多葛学派是由亚里士多德的伦理学范畴进化而来的。

亚里士多德伦理学在基督教的中世纪(5世纪至15世纪)受到了广泛的欢迎,当时有很多哲学家和宗教学者(其中著名的有13世纪的大阿尔伯特* 和托马斯·阿奎那)写了《尼各马可伦理学》评注。[4] 随后的文艺复兴时期(14—17世纪欧洲文化由于转向古典模式而复兴的时期),哲学家们对于这一著作继续予以关注。例如,哲学家弗朗西斯科·苏亚雷斯* 赞同亚里士多德的观点,认为人的本质具有普遍性的目的,而这个普遍性的目的是伦理学形成的基础。

但是,后来的哲学家们越来越不认同中世纪对于亚里士多德学派和基督教伦理学的结合。比如,英国哲学家托马斯·霍布斯*(1588—1679)认为人类所有行为都是源自于物理原因,而非根本原因或者目的原因(即人行为的目的)。他认为人的行为类似于机器的运行,而不是行使自由意志的结果。他的观点在现代哲学当中变得更加主流。[5]因此在中世纪之后的几个世纪当中,作为一个完整体系的亚里士多德伦理学受欢迎程度有所下降。但是,大约在20世纪中叶,许多哲学家返回到亚里士多德的思想,把他看做当代世界启蒙式的道德哲学家。

> "阿奎那的道德哲学有至少三个目的:1)他尝试解释亚里士多德,并说明亚里士多德的道德概念对于我们的意义。2)他试图证明这一道德概念可以用哲学的方法进行辩护。3)他试图证明这一道德概念同样可以满足神学的要求,满足基督教教义的道德要求。"
> ——特伦斯·欧文:《伦理学发展史》

思想流派

基于亚里士多德伦理学所创建的最为重要的思想派别或许是中世纪的经院哲学*。经院哲学家们翻译、评判性地解释柏拉图和亚里士多德的著述以及圣经。在这个过程中,他们尝试着把这些道德和哲学的权威资源融合起来。哲学家大阿尔伯特对亚里士多德《尼各马可伦理学》进行评述的《超级伦理学》就是一个例子。该书完成于1250年,成为中世纪创作的最有影响力的伦理学著作。[6]另一部重要的评注是托马斯·阿奎那于13世纪70年代早期完成的作品。最为重要的是,阿奎那把亚里士多德的伦理学体系纳入到他极具影响力的杰作《神学大全》(创作于1265—1274年)之中。阿奎那继承了亚里士多德的观点,认为每种德性都是恶习之间的中道。

他还认为实践理性（阿奎那用拉丁语 *prudentia* 来表示）是我们知识的源泉，告诉我们哪些行为和品质特征是德性的。[7]

特伦斯·欧文认为，阿奎那试图为亚里士多德的伦理学进行哲学的辩护，并将其和基督教的思想融合。阿奎那非常尊敬亚里士多德，欧文描述过阿奎那如何受亚里士多德的道德理论深远的影响。但是，需要指明的是，很多学者认为阿奎那在改进亚里士多德伦理学的基础上，提出了自己的哲学思想。[8] 即便如此，由于阿奎那的著作对其后的基督教神学家具有影响，我们可以说亚里士多德对于中世纪的知识和伦理的发展前景也产生了影响。

当代研究

过去的60多年里，亚里士多德伦理学对哲学研究以及现代世界所具有的现实意义重新成为人们探究的兴趣点。近年出版的两部《尼各马可伦理学》的相关文集可以说明这一点。其中一部是《剑桥〈尼各马可伦理学〉指南》，另一部是《阿奎那与〈尼各马可伦理学〉》。后者展现了从中世纪到21世纪亚里士多德对其他思想学派的影响。最近对《尼各马可伦理学》的研究兴趣的复苏，开始于英国哲学家伊丽莎白·安斯康姆1958年发表的文章《现代道德哲学》。[10] 在该文中，针对20世纪道德哲学家们对于道德理论中"道德义务"概念的混乱使用，她呼吁大家重新审视亚里士多德伦理学。安斯康姆说，这样的审视能够让我们找到对于"德性"的明确定义，并有可能带来伦理学的新见解。

此后，很多道德哲学家致力于发展以亚里士多德思想为核心的伦理学，其中最为重要的两位是苏格兰哲学家阿拉斯代尔·麦金泰尔以及新西兰哲学家罗莎琳德·赫斯特豪斯*。麦金泰尔写作了影响巨大的著作《德性之后》(又译《追寻美德》)。在书中,他指出,当代世界的特征是无休止、不连贯的伦理学争论,其源头就是现代人抛弃了亚里士多德关于人的本质的固有目的的观点[11]。麦金泰尔认为,只有通过亚里士多德伦理学的某种形式,才能回到一个更加统一的研究路径上。

同样,赫斯特豪斯在《美德伦理学》(2001)中指出,认为德性伦理学只关注个体品质的观点是错误的。德性伦理学家能够提供恰当的行为原则或规范的具体指导。赫斯特豪斯的论述提供了与德性和恶习有关的规则。正如她所言:"不仅是每一种德性会产生一个指令——行事要诚实、仁慈、慷慨等,每一种恶习也都会产生一个禁令——不要行不诚实、不仁慈、卑劣之事等。"[12] 赫斯特豪斯对于亚里士多德《尼各马可伦理学》的继承体现在两个方面,一是她强调德性,二是她坚持把德性行为作为她理论的目标。

---

1. 引自第欧根尼·拉尔修:《名哲言行录》,R. D. 希克斯编,马萨诸塞州坎布里奇:哈佛大学出版社,1966 年,x.129—32;安德鲁·赫勒查克:《幸福与希腊伦理学思想》,伦敦:康蒂纽姆出版社,2005 年,第 76 页。
2. 参见凯伦·M. 尼尔森:"希腊时期哲学中的《尼各马可伦理学》——隐藏的宝藏?",选自《亚里士多德伦理学的接受》,剑桥:剑桥大学出版社,2012 年,第 6—8 页。
3. 凯伦·M. 尼尔森:"希腊时期哲学中的《尼各马可伦理学》";安东尼·亚瑟·朗:"亚里士多德对给斯多葛学派的伦理学遗产",选自《古典研究所公报》

第 15 卷，1968 年第 1 期，第 72—85 页。

4. 安东尼·赛兰诺："论中世纪亚里士多德伦理学评注中审慎和良知与幸福的关系"，选自《亚里士多德伦理学的接受》，米勒·乔恩编，第 125—154 页，剑桥：剑桥大学出版社，2012 年。

5. 唐纳德·卢瑟福："目的之目的？近代早起伦理学中的亚里士多德主题"，选自《亚里士多德伦理学的接受》，米勒·乔恩编，第 194—221 页，剑桥：剑桥大学出版社，2012 年。

6. 安东尼·赛兰诺："论中世纪亚里士多德伦理学评注中审慎和良知与幸福的关系"；安东尼·戈捷："关于《尼各马可伦理学》的三部'阿威罗伊主义'评注"，选自《中世纪教义和文学历史档案》第 16 卷（1947—8）：第 187—336 页。

7. 詹妮弗·赫特："阿奎那关于殉道者的勇气的亚里士多德主义辩护"，选自《阿奎那与〈尼各马可伦理学〉》，托拜厄斯·霍夫曼、乔恩·穆勒和马提亚·博坎姆编，剑桥：剑桥大学出版社，2013 年，第 125 页；参见约翰·芬尼斯："阿奎那道德哲学、政治哲学和法哲学"，选自《斯坦福哲学百科词典》（2014 夏季版），登录日期 2016 年 1 月 15 日，http://plato.stanford.edu/archives/sum2014/entries/aquinas-moral-political/。

8. 对此伦理学体系的阐述及阿奎那与亚里士多德的分歧，参见约翰·芬尼斯："阿奎那道德哲学、政治哲学和法哲学"。

9. 参见罗纳德·波兰斯基编：《剑桥〈尼各马可伦理学〉指南》，剑桥：剑桥大学出版社，2014 年；《阿奎那与〈尼各马可伦理学〉》，托拜厄斯·霍夫曼、乔恩·穆勒和马提亚·博坎姆，剑桥：剑桥大学出版社，2013 年。

10. 伊丽莎白·安斯康姆："现代道德哲学"，《哲学》第 33 卷，1958 年第 124 期，第 1—19 页。

11. 参见阿拉斯代尔·麦金泰尔：《德性之后》第 3 版，诺特丹：圣母大学出版社，2007 年，第 1—3 页，第 109—120 页。

12. 罗莎琳德·赫斯特豪斯：《美德伦理学》，牛津：牛津大学出版社，2001 年，第 36 页。

11 当代印迹

要点

- 《尼各马可伦理学》是当代德性伦理学发展的关键文本。
- 德性伦理学的批评者抱怨德性不能提供充足的规则来指导行为——它只告诉你要行善事,却不告诉你如何去做。
- 德性伦理学者否认有一种伦理学体系能够具体地提供在任何情况下的明确的行事准则,从而实践智慧(*phronesis*)成为一部合适的道德哲学的必不可少的部分。

地位

亚里士多德在《尼各马可伦理学》中提出的观点是理解道德哲学史的关键。但是,从19世纪初到20世纪中叶,他的理论没有被当成实用的哲学路径。1958年,英国哲学家伊丽莎白·安斯康姆在一篇关于现代道德哲学的重要论文中对这一观点提出了挑战。[1] 她将现代道德哲学和亚里士多德伦理学思想进行了对比,认为前者没有给"道德应该"和"道德义务"前后一致的定义。[2] 她发现,亚里士多德建立了一个连贯的伦理学体系,却没有使用上述模糊的术语,而是聚焦于一些含义更为丰富的概念,如"正义"和"勇敢"等。因此,回归到亚里士多德的伦理体系,通过更新对于德性的理解,可以提供一条深化我们对于道德的理解的路径。她的这篇文章推动建立了新亚里士多德学派——由以德性伦理学为主要研究对象的现代思想家组成的学派。

20世纪80年代,阿拉斯代尔·麦金泰尔的《德性之后》(1981)

探讨了德性的本质，这是对亚里士多德关于功能（ergon）的观点的一次更新。在该书中，麦金泰尔提出，人的功能不是像亚里士多德认为的那样，由普遍的生物性目的决定，而是取决于人在社会中扮演的角色的本质。在他看来，德性是结构良好的品质特征，它们对于不同的社会实践和社会角色中的善来说是必需的。

最后，新西兰哲学家罗莎琳德·赫斯特豪斯的《美德伦理学》（2001）致力于复兴亚里士多德的德性思想。她认为德性能够对于人们在特定形势下如何行事提供指导，而恶习能够指导人们避免特定的行为。以上例子说明，在过去60余年间，出现了亚里士多德思想的复兴。

> "我在本书中详细介绍的德性伦理学……被称为'新亚里士多德主义'。称之为'新'，至少有如下原因……它的支持者们承认亚里士多德关于奴隶和女性的看法是错误的……之所以称之为'亚里士多德主义'，是因为它尽可能地贴近亚里士多德的伦理学著作。"
>
> ——罗莎琳德·赫斯特豪斯：《美德伦理学》

互动

当前亚里士多德《尼各马可伦理学》的复兴对我们今天的主流伦理学理论——如结果主义*和康德伦理学*——提出了挑战。结果主义认为，一个行为、意图或情感的善只取决于它带来的结果；而康德伦理学认为，一个行为，当且仅当它表达了一条可以被当做所有理性生物的普遍律法时，它才是正确的。[3]

20世纪前半叶，与上述两种伦理学体系相比，亚里士多德的

《尼各马可伦理学》似乎变得无足轻重。但是，得益于安斯康姆对现代道德哲学极具影响力的批判，亚里士多德的作品近年来得到了更多的关注。[4]

新亚里士多德学派的哲学家从几个方面批判结果主义和康德伦理学。

首先，他们指出品格的发展对于道德教育和伦理学反思是非常重要的。相较于只能产出指导我们执行或者避免某种行为的规则的伦理学体系，像亚里士多德那样强调德性的发展的方法更能体现我们实际的道德发展。

其次，德性伦理学家强调情感和道德生活之间的重要关系。[5] 理性主义*伦理学方法，如康德伦理学，建立在知识必然来自于理论理性的假设的基础上，常常无法理解人们在判断什么是正确的行为时对于情感的倚重。赫斯特豪斯指出，"康德伦理学中确实有很多内容"体现出他的理论"把情感排除在我们的理性本质之外"。[6] 她强调结合情感和实践理性，这是对于亚里士多德认为实践理性必须统帅我们的情感和行为的观点的发展。亚里士多德说过："德性是关于情感和行为的。"[7]

最后，德性伦理学家认为，其他的伦理学理论——如结果主义等——建立在关于人的本质或者基本价值的错误观点之上。例如，功利主义*——结果主义的一种形式——建立在我们应该在所有的行为中将快乐最大化并减少痛苦的假设之上。然而，亚里士多德曾经指出，"快乐"是一个混乱的概念。[8] 有时它指的是某种心理状态，有时它指的又是某种特定的行为。[9] 因此，我们可以把快乐看做某种事物的积极的心理副作用，我们也可以说"踢足球是我最大的快乐"。基于亚里士多德认为我们对于快乐的使用是模糊不清的这一观点，安斯康姆认为功利主义"没有注意到快乐的概念带来的困难"。[10]

因此，单单这种快乐的概念不能成为伦理学理论的基础。由于德性伦理学家的上述观点，很多结果主义和康德伦理学的支持者尝试从他们的理论体系内部提出一种对于德性和道德发展的作用的阐述。[11]

持续争议

如上所述，康德伦理学将行为的正当性建立在人们依照恰当规则行事的基础上，而结果主义则认为行为的正当性只取决于预期的结果。对于德性伦理学，特别是亚里士多德的德性伦理学，这些理论的支持者们主要提出了几大反对意见。

首先，德性伦理学，尤其是亚里士多德在《尼各马可伦理学》中所呈现的德性伦理学，似乎不能向我们提供实际的伦理学指导。亚里士多德和其拥护者认为，人类至高的善是依照德性行事。但是亚里士多德也认为，我们是通过小时候的道德教育所养成的习惯来发展道德品质的，没有这种道德教育，我们不能够成为可以认识到德性生活的善的人——因为一个人只有先具有好的品质，才能够认识到发展德性需要作出哪些努力。正如哲学家麦凯*所言，"这是一个无限循环，作用有限。"[12]

一些道德哲学家反对亚里士多德伦理学思想，因为他的德目是以他生活的时代的文化为基础的，而不是建立在永恒的、普遍的事实之上的。英国道德哲学家伯纳德·威廉斯*总结道："亚里士多德的概念和伦理思想的范式和我们今天所接受的伦理思想的范式之间有多大的差距，这个问题尚待讨论。"[13] 因此，亚里士多德学派面临着一个任务，就是解释清楚：虽然德性随着时代的改变而改变，但伦理学真理却不会变。

例如，大多数人会认为，亚里士多德认为女人（以及所有没有财产的人）不可能拥有德性的观点，是一个重大的文化盲点。但是，对于那些认为亚里士多德只是反映了他自己的文化价值观的指控，道德哲学家玛莎·努斯鲍姆进行了反击。她写道："如果我们进一步探究亚里士多德罗列和区分德性的方法，我们会注意到一些事实，这些事实对于认为他只是描述了他生活的社会当中所赞赏的美德的观点提出了质疑。"[14] 虽然亚里士多德受到了他所生活的雅典社会文化背景的影响，但他力图为最为精彩的（社会文化的）方面辩护，同时批判它的缺失。因此，我们或许可以承认他的德目不够完美，或者不具有普遍性，但这绝对不应该成为我们摒弃他的伦理生活基本方法的原因。我们应该做的，是保持一种开放的态度，如果有人提出更好的德目，那我们就修正自己的德目。[15]

---

1. 伊丽莎白·安斯康姆："现代道德哲学"，《哲学》第 33 卷，1958 年第 124 期。
2. 安斯康姆："现代道德哲学"，第 4—5 页。
3. 康德伦理学的一种版本，参见克里斯汀·科尔斯戈德：《规范性的来源》，剑桥：剑桥大学出版社，2012 年，第 19—20 页。
4. 安斯康姆："现代道德哲学"。
5. 亚里士多德：《尼各马可伦理学》，罗吉尔·克里斯普译，剑桥：剑桥大学出版社，2014 年，第 1 卷，第 8 章，1099a7—12；第 2 卷，第 6 章，1106b16—17。
6. 罗莎琳德·赫斯特豪斯：《美德伦理学》，牛津：牛津大学出版社，2001 年，第 109 页。

7. 亚里士多德:《尼各马可伦理学》,第 3 卷,第 1 章,1109b30;第 2 卷,第 5 章,1105b20。
8. 亚里士多德:《尼各马可伦理学》,第 10 卷,第 5 章,1175a23。
9. 参见安斯康姆:"现代道德哲学";阿拉斯代尔·麦金泰尔:《德性之后》,诺特丹:圣母大学出版社,2007 年,第 62—64 页。
10. 安斯康姆:"现代道德哲学",第 2 页。
11. 关于休谟与康德道德哲学,参见玛莎·努斯鲍姆:"德性伦理学:一个误导性的范畴?",《伦理学杂志》第 3 卷,1999 年第 3 期,第 163—201 页。
12. 麦凯:《伦理学:发明对与错》,伦敦:企鹅出版社,1911 年,第 186 页。
13. 伯纳德·威廉斯:《伦理学与哲学的限度》,伦敦:劳特里奇出版社,2006 年,第 49 页。
14. 玛莎·努斯鲍姆:"不相关的美德:亚里士多德主义路径",《中西部哲学研究》第 13 卷,1998 年第 1 期,第 34 页。
15. 此方法的例子参见阿拉斯代尔·麦金泰尔:《谁的正义?哪种理性?》,伦敦:达克沃斯出版社,1988 年,尤其是"传统的理性",第 349—69 页。

12 未来展望

要点

- 《尼各马可伦理学》将仍然是最具影响力的伦理学著述之一。
- 作为德性伦理学的经典文本，支持者和反对者都会继续谈及亚里士多德的《尼各马可伦理学》；他们的讨论会继续回到这本著作。
- 《尼各马可伦理学》提供了一个综合性的伦理学体系，它是很多以德性为核心的伦理学体系的基础。

潜力

《尼各马可伦理学》对于当代和未来哲学的潜在影响力，主要和德性伦理学的命运相关[1]。德性伦理学家从《尼各马可伦理学》中得到了启发和核心主题，突出了德性、幸福、实践智慧等话题。罗莎琳德·赫斯特豪斯写道："德性伦理学既是伦理学的老方法，也是新方法。'老'是因为它最早可以回溯到柏拉图甚至亚里士多德的著作；'新'是因为它作为这种古老方法的复兴，是当代道德哲学领域相对近期的一个新增内容。"[2]

目前，哲学研究对于两个问题有着持续的兴趣：一是德性伦理学是否提出了行之有效的标准道德理论的替代性选择，二是亚里士多德的德性理论是不是最好的德性伦理。

此外，有研究者致力于进一步详细阐述《尼各马可伦理学》，将它的框架和亚里士多德此前未探讨的问题联系起来。亚里士多德研究者莎拉·布罗迪*认为亚里士多德学派在这些方面应该谨慎小心。尽管"很多亚里士多德在《尼各马可伦理学》中提出的观点仍然塑造着我们自己的思想,"她写道,我们可能忽略了一个同样重要的事实——"我们自己关于伦理学的很多核心探索,都是与亚里士多德因为某种原因从未探讨过或者很少探讨的问题相关的。"[3] 针对这些问题,一些德性伦理学家给出了他们认为符合亚里士多德伦理学精神的答案。这个答案,促使学者们带着对现代德性伦理学者的关注,用全新的视角再来研读这部著作。

> "尽管亚里士多德并没有创立德性伦理学的可能性是存在的,但这种可能性和很多德性伦理学非常鲜明的新亚里士多德主义特征是冲突的。这一点,鲁思·安娜·普特南在对德性伦理学的清晰定义中表达的非常精彩:'……德性伦理学就是亚里士多德建立的。'"
> ——肖恩·麦卡尼尔:《德性伦理的一种亚里士多德式的解释》

未来方向

虽然并非所有的德性伦理学家都是新亚里士多德学派*,但德性伦理学的复兴也带来了《尼各马可伦理学》核心层面的发展。虽然很多德性伦理学家认同亚里士多德提出的善的生活由德性的行为构成的核心观点,[4] 但该书似乎是为某个特定的时期的特定社会而作——即公元前4世纪的雅典社会,因此其中的一些内容需要更新。亚里士多德的德性不一定就是我们的德性(反之亦然),[5] 比如,亚里士多德的德性中就没有涵盖我们现在与环境的互动。将来,德性伦理学将持续从德性伦理学的视角,为堕胎、安乐死、医学研究等问题提供富有成效的讨论。[6]

因为德性在伦理学发展中起着如此重要的作用,教育家们开始再次关注品质的发展。这一做法可以回溯到亚里士多德在《尼各马可伦理学》最后一卷中提出的观点：道德教育必须从小开始。[7] 一些教育学家认为，应该向孩子解释清楚特定情境之下的德性和恶习，并且鼓励德性、反对恶行。[8] 虽然亚里士多德没有涵盖我们关注的所有实践问题，《尼各马可伦理学》对于我们的时代和社会仍然有意义，仍然能提供我们发展德性的有用框架。亚里士多德研究者保拉·戈特利布*评论道："毫无疑问，即便经过了2 000多年的研究之后，亚里士多德的伦理学著作中，仍然有精华等待我们去发现，有新的富有成果的研究路径等待我们去探索。"[9]

小结

亚里士多德的《尼各马可伦理学》是一部古老的、逻辑严密的、高度原创的、开创性的讨论伦理学理论的著作。它的核心观点是人类的善是由合乎道德德性和理智德性的行为（活动）构成的。亚里士多德融合了几乎所有我们现在仍然觉得重要的伦理学理论的要素：道德品质及其养成、人类行为、情感、快乐以及德性。赫斯特豪斯将亚里士多德伦理学的影响总结如下："德性伦理学的创始人是柏拉图，或者更准确地说是亚里士多德……它至少在直到启蒙运动*之前，都是西方道德哲学中的显学。19世纪它曾一度黯淡，但又于20世纪50年代后期在英美哲学中复兴。"[10]

简而言之，亚里士多德的《尼各马可伦理学》对哲学研究有着深远的影响。

当代亚里士多德伦理学的复兴对于道德哲学有着广泛的影响，而且有迹象表明，这种影响将会持续下去。即便在同时代最具影响力的伦理学著作当中，《尼各马可伦理学》也鲜有对手。而且，这种影响并不仅仅是在学术领域。亚里士多德对于德性的强调,被应用到当代对于资本主义*的社会和经济体制的批评当中[11],被应用到环境保护[12]、医学领域的伦理问题等等当中[13]。因此,《尼各马可伦理学》仍然是——并且一直会是——哲学史上最为重要的著作之一。

---

1. 重要著作收录于:罗吉尔·克里斯普和迈克尔·斯洛特编:《德性伦理学》,牛津:牛津大学出版社,1997年。
2. 罗莎琳德·赫斯特豪斯:《美德伦理学》,牛津:牛津大学出版社,2001年,第9页。
3. 莎拉·布罗迪:"亚里士多德和当代伦理学",选自《布莱克维尔〈尼各马可伦理学〉指南》,理查德·克劳特编,牛津:威利—布莱克维尔出版社,2006年,第344。
4. 此观点及论证参见亚里士多德:《尼各马可伦理学》,大卫·罗斯译;亚里士多德:《尼各马可伦理学》,罗吉尔·克里斯普译,剑桥:剑桥大学出版社,2014年,第1卷,第7章,1098a7—20。
5. 德性的比较参见亚里士多德:《尼各马可伦理学》,第3卷,6—v.11。
6. 德性伦理学这一发展趋势的证据,参见迈克尔·奥斯丁:《行为中的德性——应用美德伦理学新命题》,纽约:帕尔格雷夫麦克米伦出版社,2013年。
7. 亚里士多德:《尼各马可伦理学》,第10卷,第9章,1179b21—1180a19。
8. 参见琳达·凯夫林·波普夫、丹·波普夫和约翰·凯夫林:《家庭美德指南:激发孩子与我们自己最好的内在品质》,纽约:普卢姆出版社,1997年;米歇尔·波巴:《建立道德智慧:教会孩子如何正确行事的七大德性》,新泽西霍博肯:乔西—巴斯出版社,2001年。
9. 保拉·戈特列布:"亚里士多德伦理学",选自《牛津伦理学史手册》,罗吉尔·克里斯普编,牛津:牛津大学出版社,2013年。

10. 罗莎琳德·赫斯特豪斯:"美德伦理学",选自《斯坦福哲学百科词典》(2013秋季版),登录日期2016年2月27日,http://plato.stanford.edu/archives/fall2013/entries/ethics-virtue/。
11. 举例参见保罗·布莱克利奇和奈特·凯文编:《德性与政治:阿拉斯代尔·麦金泰尔的革命性的亚里士多德哲学》,印第安纳诺特丹:圣母大学出版社,2011年。
12. 举例参见罗纳德·桑德勒:《品质与环境:德性为导向的环境伦理学路径》,纽约:哥伦比亚大学出版社,2007年。
13. 举例参见罗莎琳德·赫斯特豪斯:"美德理论与堕胎",《哲学与公共事务》第20卷,1991年第3期,第223—46页。

术语表

1. **阿卡德米**：柏拉图于公元前385年左右在雅典创办的哲学和数学研究机构（也叫柏拉图学园）。

2. **意志薄弱（*Akrasia*）**：希腊语，意为"意志薄弱"或"缺乏掌控力"。英语中常翻译为"incontinence"（失禁）。意志薄弱是看似知道如何正确行事，却不能正确行事的人的性格特征。

3. **回廊**：有顶棚遮盖的、可供人们来回散步的区域。

4. **勇气（*Andreia*）**：希腊语。出现于柏拉图的著作中，常被翻译为"勇气"。

5. **人类学**：研究人的本质的学科。"人类学"是关于人类是什么的一系列观念，通常也包括什么使人类繁荣兴盛的观念。

6. **德性（*Aretê*）**：希腊语，字面意义为"优秀"。在柏拉图和亚里士多德的著作中，常翻译为"德性"。

7. **生物学**：对所有类型的有机生命的系统研究。亚里士多德的生物学研究的核心，是观察和分类多种海洋生物、植物和哺乳类动物。

8. **资本主义**：在现代西方占据优势的社会和经济体制，工业和贸易由私人控制，为私人获利。

9. **结果主义**：结果主义伦理学以行为的后果判断它的道德性。

10. **沉思**：对于永恒真理的理性反思。亚里士多德认为，沉思是人最好的活动，是把人和动物区分开来、使人更接近于神的特性。

11. **全集**：一位作家一生中所创作的所有书面作品的集合。

12. **民主**：公民个体通过投票决定法律和代表来统治的政治组织形式。该词来自于希腊语，意为"人民的权力"。

13. **正义（*Dikaiosune*）**：古希腊词语，指正义的德性。

14. **主义**：哲学的主义是哲学家深信不疑的观点；哲学"主义"可以通过推理和论证而推翻。

15. **公认观点**(*Endoxa*)：亚里士多德使用的一个术语，指大多数人所共有的、经过时间考验的观点。公认观点是道德哲学的出发点，道德哲学的任务是用连贯的理论阐述公认的意见。

16. **启蒙运动**：西方世界知识和文化得到快速、广泛的发展的一段时期，约公元1650—1800年；引发了哲学、政治学、经济学和社会的重大发展。

17. **伊壁鸠鲁学派**：古代重要的哲学流派之一，由伊壁鸠鲁（公元前341—270年）建立。其主要特征为唯物主义和把快乐看作最高的善。

18. **功能**(*Ergon*)：古希腊词语，意为"功能"。本概念是亚里士多德认为人类的功能决定伦理生活本质这一观点的基础。

19. **伦理学**：哲学的分支学科，回答"人应该如何生活"的问题。关注的核心概念常包括正当和不正当的行为、美德和道德义务。

20. **幸福**(*Eudaimonia*)：亚里士多德提出的人的生命和活动都指向的目标。常被翻译为"幸福"或者"福祉"，但其真实含义介乎于这两者之间："幸福"是一种有意识的人类才能拥有的状态；"福祉"是某种生活的客观质量。

21. **享乐**(*Hedone*)：希腊词语，意为"快乐"。享乐主义（hedonism）——以享乐为所有事情的目的——就源自于该词。

22. **希腊时期**（公元前322年—公元前31年）：古希腊文化和政治发展壮大的一个历史时期，结束于公元前31年，古希腊被罗马帝国取代。

23. **意志薄弱**：希腊词语 *akrasia* 的常见英语译文，意为"意志薄弱"或"缺乏掌控力"——意志薄弱是看似知道如何正确行事，却不能正确行事的人的性格特征。

24. **康德伦理学**：继承18世纪哲学家伊曼努尔·康德思想的伦理学体系。致力于提出行为的普遍规则，认为人们不普遍意愿的行为是不道德的。

25. **逻辑学**：哲学的分支学科，由亚里士多德开创，研究演绎推理和归纳推理的本质和依据。亚里士多德的逻辑学专注于术语之间的严格的逻辑关系，但自亚里士多德之后逻辑学变得更加广泛。

26. **吕克昂**：亚里士多德创建的哲学学校，他的数部著作写作于此。学校位于雅典，在亚里士多德逝世后仍然继续存在。

27. **中道**：数学术语，指两个极端值之间的中数。本书中脱离了数学的含义，指令人满意的中间立场。

28. **中世纪**：西欧历史上从公元 500 年至 1500 年的一段时期，始于罗马帝国的衰落。这一时期，罗马天主教教义和亚里士多德的思想都对政治学、科学、哲学等领域产生了重大的影响。

29. **豪迈**（*Megalopsuchia*）：字面意思为"灵魂的伟大"——亚里士多德伦理学体系中最高的德性，指一个拥有所有其他德性、对此有自我认识且注重自身荣誉表现的人的品质特征。

30. **形而上学**：研究实体本质的哲学分支学科。字面意思为"物理学之后"，因为亚里士多德关于实体本质的著作排在关于物理学的著作之后。

31. **道德哲学**：既研究理论道德又研究实践道德的哲学分支学科。主要回答"什么是善的生活的本质"和"我们应该如何生活"等问题。

32. **新亚里士多德派学者**：20 世纪致力于复兴亚里士多德思想的一群学者。他们相信德性伦理学——认为德性在人的行为和对于行动的道德判断中发挥重要的作用。

33. **伯罗奔尼撒战争**（公元前 431 年—公元前 404 年）：雅典城邦及其盟军和斯巴达城邦及其盟军之间的战争，斯巴达人获胜。希腊历史上最长的战争冲突，最终导致希腊各城邦的削弱，并在公元前 1 世纪面对外来势力时落败。

34. **逍遥学派**：亚里士多德的追随者。常与希腊词语 *peripatos*（散步）一起被提及，可能源于吕克昂学园附近的回廊——有顶棚遮盖的可供散步的地方。

35. **波斯战争**：公元前 499 年至公元前 448 年之间，波斯帝国和希腊城邦联盟之间的战争。实力占优的波斯帝国数次试图攻占雅典，均以失败告终。

36. **现象**（*Phainomena*）：希腊语，意为"外观"，或者看上去似乎如此的事物。亚里士多德把现象和公认观点作为他的哲学研究的出发点。

37. **《斐利布斯篇》**：柏拉图晚期对话录之一，探讨快乐和知识对于善的生活的意义。对话中的人物有苏格拉底、普逻达查斯和斐利布斯。

38. **哲学**：将抽象推理和实践推理应用到人生活中的问题当中的学科。研究的问题有："我们如何知道真理？"、"什么是善的生活？"、"真实的现实是什么样的？"等。

39. **实践智慧**（*Phronesis*）：希腊语，意为"实践智慧"或"谨慎"。亚里士多德认为实践智慧是一种理智德性，能够帮助我们判断特定情境中正当的行为。

40. **城邦/城市**（*Polis*）：希腊语，意为"城市"。常指古希腊城邦，如雅典和斯巴达。

41. **前苏格拉底哲学**：指从米利都的泰勒斯（约公元前624年—公元前546年）时期开始，到苏格拉底之前的哲学家们。包括米利都学派、毕达哥拉斯学派、埃利亚学派、原子论学派，以及哲学家赫拉克利特、阿那克萨哥拉等。他们研究的兴趣都在于探究自然世界的本质。

42. **目的原因**：以产生某个具体的结果为目的的原因。亚里士多德将这类原因称之为"根本原因"。

43. **理性主义**：强调知识依赖于理论理性的流派。

44. **理性**：人类进行抽象思维的能力。理性可以是理论性的，也可以是实践性的；可以处理观念之间的关系，也可以处理事实之间的关系。

45. **文艺复兴**：西欧历史上从大约15世纪到17世纪早期的一段时期，意为"重生"。在这一时期内，哲学家、艺术家、作家等重新发现和使用了古希腊、古罗马古典时期的许多伟大的文学和艺术作品。

46. **修辞学**：使用语言进行说服的艺术。现代常含贬义（空洞的花言巧语），但历史上其含义为好的论证和批判性的思维。

47. **罗马时期**（公元前27年—公元395年）：古罗马成为强大的、统治欧洲大部的帝国的一段历史时期。

48. **经院哲学**：中世纪统治西方哲学的哲学研究传统。经院哲学（以及经院哲学家）吸收了柏拉图和亚里士多德的著作中的大量内容，寻求哲学和罗马天主教神学的融合。

49. **怀疑主义学派**：古代重大哲学流派之一，通常认为开端于爱里斯的皮浪（公元前365年—公元前275年）。怀疑主义学派历史上有多次变化，但一般都认为没有任何事物是确定、可知的。

50. **智慧**（*Sophia*）：希腊语，意为"智慧"。亚里士多德用此概念来指能够帮助我们发现最为高贵和光荣的真理的理性能力，而真理是哲学家全身心地追求的。

51. **智者**：古希腊时期的职业教师，致力于掌握从修辞学到音乐等几种学科的优秀技能。柏拉图（或许不太公正地）将智者刻画为"爱钱财者"，而不是为了智慧而热爱智慧的人，并且认为他们只追求说服别人，而不是发现真理。

52. **节制**（*Sophrosune*）：希腊语，意为"节制"。柏拉图伦理学著作中的美德之一。

53. **斯巴达**：古希腊城邦之一，位于伯罗奔尼撒（今希腊南部半岛）。斯巴达和雅典都是古代世界最为强大的希腊城邦。

54. **斯多葛学派**：古代伟大的哲学流派之一，或许是最具影响力的一个学派。公元前3世纪早期由基提翁的芝诺创立于雅典。有很强的道德维度，认为美德是获得幸福的充足条件。

55. **目的论的**：与目的或构思相关的。

56. **节制**：在恰当的情境中恰当地约束享乐的心理倾向。

57. **专著**：系统、彻底地描述和分析某一主题的书面作品。

58. **功利主义**：19世纪英国思想家杰里米·边沁（1748—1832）创立的道德哲学流派，认为道德的善只在于最大多数的人最大化的快乐和最小化的痛苦。

59. **德性伦理学**：也叫"基于德性的伦理学"或者"基于主体的伦理学"，认为行为的道德性取决于人的品质或者德性，而不是行为的结果（后者即"结果主义伦理学"）。

60. **德性**：部分地构成人善的生活并使其为可能的品质和行为倾向。德性是几乎所有古代道德哲学体系的重要内容，古代哲学家们共同强调的德性有实践智慧、勇敢、节制和正义。

61. **西方世界**：以欧洲和北美为核心的文化，古希腊、古罗马、基督教等文化是其重要源头。

人名表

1. **阿佛洛狄西亚的亚历山大**：亚里士多德学派哲学家,曾主持雅典阿卡德米学园,毕生致力于以数量众多的亚里士多德著作评注来支持亚里士多德哲学,反对柏拉图哲学。

2. **亚历山大大帝**(公元前356年—公元前323年):马其顿国王腓力二世的儿子,登上王位后,发动了史无前例的军事行动,征服了波斯和埃及,到达印度,缔造了古代最为庞大的帝国之一。

3. **罗得岛的安德罗尼柯**:很有可能是第一部可靠的亚里士多德著作的编注者。安德罗尼柯可能是雅典吕克昂学园的领袖之一,但几乎没有关于他在何时任职的具体证据。

4. **伊丽莎白·安斯康姆**(1919—2001):英国分析哲学家。她的研究领域广泛,包括心灵哲学、逻辑学、伦理学等,对德性伦理学的发展做出了决定性的贡献。

5. **托马斯·阿奎那**(1225—1274):意大利神学家、哲学家,多明我会成员。他可能是中世纪最为重要的哲学家。在数量众多的作品中,他融合了亚里士多德哲学和基督教神学。

6. **奥古斯特·伊曼努尔·贝克**(1785—1871):德国哲学家、编辑。创立了亚里士多德著作的贝克编号系统。

7. **克里斯·波波尼奇**(1960年生):美国哲学家,研究重心为古代哲学,特别是柏拉图哲学。

8. **莎拉·布罗迪**(1941年生):圣安德鲁斯大学道德哲学教授,作品主要是关于古典哲学、形而上学和伦理学的。

9. **尼古拉·哥白尼**(1473—1543):波兰天文学家、数学家,著名的《天体运行论》的作者。在欧洲思想文化历史最关键的时期,他提出了以太阳为中心的宇宙模型,对科学革命作出了巨大贡献。

10. **勒内·笛卡尔**(1596—1650):法国哲学家,现代哲学奠基者。笛卡尔提出了系统怀疑的哲学方法，他最著名的作品有《方法论》（又译《谈谈方法》）(1637)和《第一哲学沉思集》(1641)。

11. 恩培多克勒（约公元前490—公元前430年）：希腊哲学家，提出四根说（气、火、水、土）来解释自然现象。

12. 伊壁鸠鲁（公元前341—公元前270年）：伊壁鸠鲁学派创始人，希腊哲学家。他在雅典建立了"花园哲学"流派，并终生于此处进行哲学思考，用信件的形式写下他的哲学思想。

13. 欧多克索斯（公元前408—355年）：希腊天文学家、数学家，柏拉图的学生，伟大的古典数学家之一。

14. 菲利帕·福特（1920—2010）：英国哲学家，因其德性伦理学作品而著名。

15. 多罗西娅·弗雷德（1941年生）：古典哲学专家，加州大学伯克利分校米尔斯兼职教授，汉堡大学荣誉教授，主要著作是关于柏拉图、亚里士多德和马丁·海德格尔的。

16. 伽利略·伽利雷（1564—1642）：意大利天文学家、数学家，科学革命主要人物之一。伽利略第一个观测到木星卫星，他还发展了近代力学。他为地球绕太阳运动的正确观点辩护，并因此受到罗马天主教会的迫害。

17. 保拉·戈特利布：威斯康星大学哲学教授，研究重点为亚里士多德伦理学和形而上学。

18. 赫拉克利特（约公元前535—公元前475年）：希腊哲学家。他用简短、晦涩的语句记录自己的哲学思想，坚持自然世界不断流变的观点。

19. 托马斯·霍布斯（1588—1679）：英国伟大哲学家，因其政治哲学著作——享有盛誉的《利维坦》(1651)而著名。

20. 大卫·休谟（1711—1776）：苏格兰哲学家、历史学家，在淡化亚里士多德思想的影响方面发挥了重要的作用。

21. 罗莎琳德·赫斯特豪斯（1943年生）：新西兰哲学家，沿袭她的老师安斯康姆和福特的路径，发展德性伦理学。

22. **特伦斯·欧文**（1947年生）：牛津大学古代哲学教授，研究重点是古代世界伦理学发展。

23. **伊曼努尔·康德**（1724—1804）：德国启蒙哲学家，写作了著名的《纯粹理性批判》和《实践理性批判》，开创了康德学派，极大地影响了德国唯心主义和伦理学。

24. **阿拉斯代尔·麦金泰尔**（1929年生）：苏格兰哲学家，伦敦都市大学高级研究员，1981年出版的著作《德性之后》（又译《追寻德性》）被公认为开创性的作品。

25. **麦凯**（1917—1981）：澳大利亚哲学家，专注于道德哲学和政治哲学的研究，最重要的著作包括《有神论的奇迹》（1982）和《伦理学：发明对与错》（1977）。

26. **大阿尔伯特**（1200—1280）：名字来源于拉丁语 Albertus Magnus，是中世纪最重要的罗马天主教哲学家、神学家之一。他促进了亚里士多德的教义和天主基督教教义的融合，最重要的作品包括两部亚里士多德《尼各马可伦理学》的评注。

27. **玛莎·努斯鲍姆**（1947年生）：美国哲学家，研究领域包括古代哲学、政治哲学、女性主义、动物权利等，在学术界内外均有极大的影响力。

28. **巴门尼德**（出生于约公元前540年）：希腊哲学家，最具影响力的前苏格拉底学派哲学家之一。他认为所有实在都是形而上地统一的，区别只在于表象。

29. **柏拉图**（公元前427—公元前347年）：希腊哲学家，雅典阿卡德米（又译"柏拉图学园"）创始人，西方最伟大的哲学家之一，苏格拉底的学生，亚里士多德的老师。他创作了伟大的《对话录》（含《理想国》和《会饮篇》），奠定了西方哲学的基础。

30. **罗纳德·波兰斯基**（1949年生）：杜肯大学哲学教授，期刊《古代哲学》编辑。

31. **安东尼·佩鲁斯**：宾汉姆顿大学哲学教授，讲授古代哲学和亚里士多德、柏拉图、苏格拉底作品等课程。

32. 苏格拉底（公元前469—公元前399年）：雅典哲学家，柏拉图的老师，于公元前399年被指控另立新神和腐蚀青年并判处死刑。苏格拉底没有留下任何文字著述，柏拉图阐述了他寻找事物准确定义的哲学方法，被公认为对西方哲学产生了关键影响。

33. 斯珀西波斯（约公元前408—公元前339年）：希腊哲学家，柏拉图的外甥，柏拉图学园的第一位院长继任者。

34. 弗朗西斯科·苏亚雷斯（1548—1617）：极具影响力的西班牙神学家、哲学家，著名作品有《形而上学的争论》（1597）和《论法律》（1612）。

35. 泰奥弗拉斯托斯（约公元前371—公元前287年）：希腊哲学家，亚里士多德的学生，吕克昂学园院长继任者。

36. 伯纳德·威廉斯（1929—2003）：影响巨大的20世纪后半叶英国道德哲学家，重要作品包括《伦理学与哲学的限度》（1985）和《功利主义：赞成和反对》（1973）。

WAYS IN TO THE TEXT

KEY POINTS

- Aristotle was born in 384 B.C.E. in Stagira, Greece. He is one of the greatest philosophers* in history.

- In his *Nicomachean Ethics*, composed between 335 and 322 B.C.E., Aristotle argues that happiness is the greatest good, and that real happiness is achieved by ethically* good action ("ethics" is the branch of philosophy concerned with the question "How should one live?").

- Aristotle's *Nicomachean Ethics* stresses that ethically good action springs from the virtues* (a term referring to dispositions of character and action) of moral character and intellect.

Who Was Aristotle?

Aristotle, the author of *Nicomachean Ethics* (composed between 335 and 322 B.C.E.), was a philosopher of ancient Greece. One of the most famous thinkers of all time, he was born in Stagira, a town in Macedonia, a kingdom north of classical Greece. Aristotle's father was a physician named Nicomachus; his mother was named Phaestis. When Aristotle turned 18, he moved to Athens, the center of learning in the Greek world, where he studied with the great philosopher Plato* at the Academy*—Plato's famed center of philosophical learning. Aristotle remained at the Academy until 348 B.C.E., and in 343 B.C.E. became the personal tutor to the young Alexander the Great.* Son of King Philip II of Macedonia, Alexander became a military leader and ruler of an enormous empire incorporating Greece.

On his return to Athens, Aristotle established his own school for the education of notable youth, the Lyceum,* in 335 B.C.E.; on account of the *peripatos*, a circular place for walking, nearby, Aristotle's followers are often called Peripatetics.* During his time as master of the Lyceum school, Aristotle lectured his students on a wide range of subjects, including politics, physics, poetry, and logic* (the subfield of philosophy concerned with methodical, rational reasoning). After a long and productive career, he died at the age of 62 on the Greek island of Euboea, in 322 B.C.E.

Aristotle devoted his life to learning, investigating nature, and passing on this knowledge to students. His status as one of the most important thinkers of all time is largely due to the survival of some of his most influential and systematic philosophical works. He also created two new fields: logic and biology* (the study of living things). Much of Aristotle's work focused on ethics, or the study of right and wrong, and *Nicomachean Ethics*, named after his father, is a timeless philosophical classic. As one commentator has noted,"Aristotle holds a position of unparalleled importance in the history of philosophy—and he is a thunderingly good philosopher to boot."[1] Many of the moral concepts and principles of what we now think of as the West* (primarily Europe, North America, and Australia-New Zealand) can be traced back to *Nicomachean Ethics*, and to the Aristotelian concepts of happiness, virtue, and practical wisdom.

What Does *Nicomachean Ethics* Say?

Although now considered one of history's first great ethical treatises* (systematic written analyses), *Nicomachean Ethics* was not published by Aristotle himself. Rather, one of Aristotle's students is likely to have organized it from a set of lecture notes Aristotle wrote for the Lyceum between 335 and 322 B.C.E. In any case, the work has profoundly influenced every era of moral philosophy* since Aristotle's day ("moral philosophy" is the branch of philosophy concerned with the theory and practice of morality—that is, with the question "How ought we to live?").

Most current editions of *Nicomachean Ethics* include 10 books and chapter divisions within the books. The division into books goes back to the oldest known versions of *Nicomachean Ethics*, but the chapters are more modern subdivisions. When the work is cited as *Nicomachean Ethics*, the citation is split into two parts, commonly taking the form "X.7.1177a13–18"; in this example, the first part ("X.7") refers to Book 10 and chapter 7 in the translation by the scholar Roger Crisp;[2] often this will be the only citation given. When the second part is used ("1177a13–18"), it corresponds to the text citation system devised by the German philosopher August Immanuel Bekker* in 1831. Using the second part, a student should be able to find the passage in virtually any translation of Aristotle's works.

Nicomachean Ethics investigates the question of what a good human life is. In answering this question, Aristotle argues that a good life is one conducted according to the function or purpose (Greek: *ergon*)* of human nature.

In Aristotle's sense, a "function" is a thing's unique and defining purpose. The function of a knife, for example, is to cut, and the function of a hammer is to hit things. Aristotle asks himself the following question: "What is the function of human beings?"—in other words, what are human beings meant to do?

Aristotle believes that mankind's highest function is *eudaimonia**—happiness, or flourishing. But what does this happiness consist of?

For Aristotle, our function as human beings will be determined by what separates us from other things in the world: reason* (the human faculty of abstract reflection). As human beings, we can exercise reason regarding both theoretical and practical matters. So, our function—and therefore the key to real *eudaimonia*—is to be realized through the proper exercise of theoretical and practical reason.

For Aristotle, the proper exercise of theoretical and practical reason was a question of recognizing the middle way between extremes of action and character; practical reason demands that people be neither cowardly nor rash in the face of danger. The mean* (that is, the desired middle) between these two extremes is the character trait of courage. These "middle way" character traits are called "virtues," and Aristotle outlines many, including justice, courage, temperance* (that is, restraint, usually with regard to pleasurable activities), and practical wisdom.

Aristotle does not omit a discussion of theoretical reason. Toward the end of *Nicomachean Ethics*, he returns to contemplation* (for him, reflection on eternal truths), a practice he considers the highest realization of *eudaimonia*. He writes in Book X.7–8: "If happiness is activity in accordance with virtue, it is reasonable to expect that it is in accordance with the highest virtue ... [T]his activity is that of contemplation."³

It is best to consider the central social or political aspect of *Nicomachean Ethics* as continuous with Aristotle's other major work on practical matters, *Politics*. In that work, Aristotle produces the famous definition of man as a "political animal" (*Politics*, 1253a1–4): our lives are social by nature, and we need the companionship of other humans to achieve happiness.⁴ Further, the goal of a group of individuals runs parallel to the goal of the individual. So the noble goal of politicians ought to be producing the material conditions for the well-being and happiness of the citizens, just as the goal of the individual is to attain the virtues necessary for his own happiness.

Why Does *Nicomachean Ethics* Matter?

The impact of *Nicomachean Ethics* and of Aristotle's arguments is perhaps unparalleled in the history of philosophy. The philosophy professor Terence Irwin* of Oxford University has said that "we can follow one significant thread through the history of moral philosophy by considering how far Aristotle is right, and what his successors think about his claims."⁵ Aristotle was called simply "the Philosopher" by medieval* thinkers. Even today, his ideas stand the test of time. Virtue ethics*—a branch of ethics that principally focuses on moral character—is now a leading current in contemporary moral philosophy.⁶ The philosopher Rosalind Hursthouse* of New Zealand has written, "Virtue ethics is both an old and a new approach to ethics, old in so far as it dates back to the writings of Plato and, more particularly, Aristotle, new in that, as a revival of this ancient approach, it is a fairly recent addition to contemporary moral theory."[7]

Nicomachean Ethics is not important only for those engaged in academic philosophy. For Aristotle, philosophy begins "because of wonder."[8] There is perhaps no more wondrous set of questions for human beings than that which *Nicomachean Ethics* addresses: What is the nature of happiness or flourishing? How do human beings achieve happiness? And why do human beings fail to achieve happiness? These universal and deeply humane questions guarantee the text's continuing importance.

Finally, when considered together with Aristotle's *Politics*, *Nicomachean Ethics* is still relevant to enduring questions in political and social science. While Aristotle wrote for a culture very different from contemporary global societies, his work can still speak meaningfully to us today; his ethical thought provides a contrast to our modern social and political assumptions. Aristotle is therefore a powerful conversation partner, offering a different perspective on even the most pressing political and economic problems of the contemporary world.[9]

---

1. J. Barnes, *The Cambridge Companion to Aristotle* (Cambridge: Cambridge University Press, 1995), xv.
2. Aristotle, *Nicomachean Ethics*, rev. ed., trans. Roger Crisp (Cambridge: *Cambridge University Press*, 2014).
3. Aristotle, *Nicomachean Ethics*, X.7.1177a.13–18.
4. Aristotle, Politics, trans. T. Irwin, in *Readings in Ancient Greek Philosophy*, eds. S. Cohen, P. Curd

and C. D. C. Reeve (Indianapolis: Hackett, 2005), 1253a1–4.
5. T. Irwin, *The Development of Ethics*, vol. 1 (Oxford: Oxford University Press, 2007), 4.
6. Rosalind Hursthouse, "Virtue Ethics," section 2, in *Stanford Encyclopedia of Philosophy*, ed. Edward N. Zalta (Fall 2013 edn.), accessed February 27, 2016, http://plato.stanford.edu/archives/fall2013/entries/ethics-virtue/.
7. Rosalind Hursthouse, *On Virtue Ethics* (Oxford: Oxford University Press, 2001), 9.
8. Aristotle, *Metaphysics*, trans. S. M. Cohen, in *Readings in Ancient Greek Philosophy*, 982b10–15.
9. For a discussion of Aristotle and how his ethics can be revolutionary even today, see Paul Blackledge and Kelvin Knight (eds.), *Virtue and Politics: Alasdair MacIntyre's Revolutionary Aristotelianism* (Notre Dame, IN: University of Notre Dame Press, 2011).

SECTION 1
INFLUENCES

MODULE 1
THE AUTHOR AND THE HISTORICAL CONTEXT

KEY POINTS

- Dealing with human happiness, Aristotle's *Nicomachean Ethics* is one of the foundational works in moral philosophy.*
- After studying for 20 years with the enormously influential thinker Plato,* Aristotle wrote groundbreaking works of his own.
- A key figure in the intellectual world of ancient Greece, Aristotle taught the military leader Alexander the Great,* who later became ruler of a vast empire.

Why Read this Text?

Aristotle, the author of *Nicomachean Ethics* (composed between 335 and 322 B.C.E.), once asserted that philosophy begins "because of wonder"[1]—the wonder, that is, that we feel in response to the puzzles presented to us in the physical world, in the social world, and in the world of individual human action.

In the text, Aristotle explores some of the most immediate and intimate sources of wonder for human beings—the question of the essential nature and purpose of human beings and the question of how we ought to live. One significant reason to read Aristotle on ethics* is that the text has long been considered foundational for the tradition of ethical reflection in Western thought.

During the Middle Ages* (the fifth to fifteenth centuries C.E.), philosophers usually referred to Aristotle simply as "the Philosopher."

Nicomachean Ethics is one of the most influential texts in ethics, and a major new commentary appears approximately every 10 years. This makes it one of the most studied and influential works in the history of Western philosophy. *Nicomachean Ethics* is the first surviving work that systematically investigates the central ethical concerns of human life: What is happiness (*eudaimonia*)* and how can it be achieved?² The work established moral philosophy as an independent discipline, and it decisively influenced the field's terminology, main arguments, and structure.

If it is clear that basic needs must be met in order to live, what is it that makes a life *good*? While everyone in Aristotle's day agreed that happiness makes for a good life, there was disagreement about what happiness is. While many considered happiness a matter of pleasure, honor, or wealth, Aristotle followed his teacher, the influential philosopher Plato, in arguing that this was a mistaken idea. Those things are sought as a means to some other end—but the ultimate goal of all human action is the good that people are really aiming at in all of their activities.

Nicomachean Ethics has maintained its relevance in every historical period and has influenced philosophical and political thought up to the present day.

> "We had perhaps better consider the universal good and discuss thoroughly what is meant by it."
> —— Aristotle, *Nicomachean Ethics*

Author's Life

Aristotle was born in 384 B.C.E. in the town of Stagira in what was then known as Macedonia, now a region of northern Greece. His father, Nicomachus, was a physician at the Macedonian court. Nicomachus gave his son the best education available and, being a physician, may have influenced the empirical, scientific emphasis in Aristotle's philosophical work ("empiricism" is an approach to scientific inquiry founded on information verifiable by observation).

At the age of 17, Aristotle went to Athens to study with Plato at his school, the Academy.*[3] He left Athens after Plato's death in 347 B.C.E., and between 347 and 343 B.C.E. he engaged in biological* studies in Asia Minor (modern-day Turkey) and the Aegean islands east of Greece. While living on the Island of Lesbos, Aristotle married a woman named Pythias; the two had a daughter by the same name. He then moved to the Macedonian court, serving for a short time as tutor to Alexander the Great. On his return to Athens in 335 B.C.E., Aristotle founded his own philosophical school, the Lyceum.* Members of this school are known as "Peripatetics," a name derived from the Greek *peripatos* ("ambulatory"),* referring to the covered walking area nearby. Aristotle produced most of his works at the Lyceum and taught there until Alexander's death in 323 B.C.E. Because of his well-known association with the Macedonians, and fearing the anti-Macedonian movement, Aristotle then left Athens, this time for good. He spent the last year of his life on the large Greek island of Euboea, where he died in 322 B.C.E.[4]

Author's Background

Aristotle lived in the ancient Greek city-state (Greek: *polis*)* of Athens for the most important part of his philosophical career. Athens was the most powerful of the hundreds of Greek city-states dotted around the Aegean Sea, and it had survived both the Persian Wars* of the early fifth century B.C.E. and the Peloponnesian War* of the late fifth century B.C.E.—conflicts that deeply shaped the region. Athens is known as the birthplace of democracy*—a system in which rule is in the hands of the people, rather than in the hands of any monarch or elite—but, in practice, only relatively wealthy male citizens were allowed to take part in the political process.

Aristotle lived in Athens during a period of relative political stability and immense cultural advances. Athens' political stability was arguably due to the success of the democratic system in the 80 years following the Peloponnesian War against the rival city-state of Sparta.* This period of general tolerance for both democrats and citizens favoring rule by the elite, provided very important stability for the development of philosophical schools. This was in spite of the fact that in 399 B.C.E. an Athenian jury put to death the influential philosopher Socrates,* who had been the teacher of Aristotle's own teacher Plato, for his "corrupting" philosophical teachings. This famous incident was an important exception to the general rule of tolerance in Athens in the fourth century B.C.E.

Due in part to this political stability, Athens had reached perhaps the highest point in its cultural development, with its most famous artists, sculptors, dramatists, and philosophers working in the fifth and fourth centuries B.C.E. It was within this context that both Plato's Academy and Aristotle's Lyceum flourished. The former was vital for Aristotle's philosophical education, and the latter was necessary for developing and passing on his own philosophical teaching. It was only when Alexander the Great died in 323 B.C.E. that the situation in Athens became a problem for Aristotle; Athenians were wary of their Macedonian neighbors to the north, and the death of Alexander meant that the stability of his empire was no longer a certainty. Tradition holds that Aristotle fled Athens in order that it might not "sin twice" against philosophy by taking his life, having already taken the life of Socrates.

Aristotle's contributions to Athens' philosophical legacy are impressive, as is his advancement of human knowledge more generally. He structured the discipline of philosophy as we know it today,[5] and he established at least two fundamental branches of science: logic* and biology.[6]

---

1. Aristotle, *Metaphysics*, trans. S. M. Cohen, in *Readings in Ancient Greek Philosophy*, eds. S. Cohen, P. Curd and C. D. C. Reeve (Indianapolis, IN: Hackett, 2005), 982b10–15.
2. Richard Kraut, "Two Conceptions of Happiness," *The Philosophical Review 88* (1979): 167–97.
3. Christopher Shields, "Aristotle," in *Stanford Encyclopedia of Philosophy,* ed. Edward N. Zalta (Fall 2015 edn.), accessed January 19, 2016, http://plato.stanford.edu/archives/fall2015/entries/aristotle/.
4. For a short version of the biography, see J. Barnes, *The Cambridge Companion to Aristotle* (Cambridge: Cambridge University Press, 1995), 1–15.
5. Especially important are his works *Physics*, *On the Soul*, and *Metaphysics*, all found in translation in Jonathan Barnes, *Aristotle Complete Works* (Princeton, NJ: Princeton University Press, 1991).
6. Georgios Anagnostopoulos, "Aristotle's Works and the Development of His Thought," in *A Companion to Aristotle*, ed. Georgios Anagnostopoulos (Oxford: Wiley-Blackwell, 2009).

MODULE 2
ACADEMIC CONTEXT

KEY POINTS

* Aristotle's *Nicomachean Ethics* is the most important and influential work in the field of moral philosophy.*
* The question of what makes a happy life is a central concern to politicians, intellectuals, and ordinary people.
* Aristotle's method is to take popular and traditional accounts of the good life seriously, and to assess them philosophically.

The Work in Its Context

Aristotle's *Nicomachean Ethics* appeared at a crucial time in the history of philosophy,* and contributes much to what we call philosophy today. While Greek culture was advanced in many fields—notably literature (poetry, epic, theatre), history, science (geometry, mathematics), music, and architecture—the discipline of philosophy was not yet fully formed. The most important forms of philosophical discussions were the oral (spoken) tradition, famously represented by the philosopher Socrates* (the influential teacher of Aristotle's teacher Plato),* and philosophical poetry, represented by the thinker Heraclitus.* Plato was the first to write extensively on philosophy in the form of dialogues (roughly, narratives of ideas conducted through characters speaking to each other), usually with Socrates as the leading character. Philosophy gradually became a discipline independent from literature and poetry; it addressed many of the same problems (life, death, happiness, the origin and nature of the world, ethics,* the immortality of the soul), but approached them more rigorously and methodically.

There were three main philosophical schools in Greek philosophy before Aristotle: the Pre-Socratics* (given that name because they pre-dated Socrates); the Sophists* (travelling professional teachers who engaged in public debates on justice, duty, happiness, and civic virtue); and the philosophical tradition of Socrates and Plato—centered at Plato's Academy.* The Pre-Socratics famously investigated nature in their search for the fundamental principles of all things.[1] Some of the more notable Pre-Socratics included the philosophers Heraclitus, Parmenides,* and Empedocles.* Socrates was the first to define philosophy as focused on problems. He did this largely by challenging the Sophists, who were more confident in their assertions about justice and virtue than was justified; while he explored many of the same civic themes as the Sophists, he did so with a critical and humble attitude.

The historian of philosophy Anthony Preus* argues that there was a key turn from Socrates onwards: "Aristotle, inventor of the word 'ethics,' says that 'in time of Socrates, people turned from inquiry into nature, and philosophers turned to political studies and the useful virtues*.'"[2] In other words, the shift from the Pre-Socratics, through the Sophists, to the intellectual approach of Socrates, Plato, and Aristotle was a shift from speculation about the original principles of nature to discussions about the ethical life.

> "It is now so widely taken for granted that 'ethics' (or 'moral philosophy' as it is sometimes called) is the name of a distinct branch of philosophy that we must constantly force ourselves to remember that this way of carving up the subject had to be invented, and that Aristotle was one of its inventors."
> —— Richard Kraut, Introduction to *The Blackwell Guide to Aristotle's Nicomachean Ethics*

Overview of the Field

Plato's *Republic* was the most important work of moral philosophy before Aristotle. As in most of Plato's dialogues, he has Socrates making the most interesting arguments, and it is often difficult to tell which ideas originate from Socrates and which are the invention of his student, Plato. In *Republic*, Plato explores the virtues in the individual person by first describing the virtues in the ideal society. He divides this imaginary society into the ruler class, the soldier class, and the citizen class. As the roles of classes of people in the well-ordered city correspond to specific virtues, the rulers of the city must be endowed with wisdom (*sophia*);* the protectors of the city, or soldiers, must have courage (*andreia*);* and the members of every class are to possess temperance or moderation (*sophrosune*)* and justice (*dikaiosune*).* The individual, in Plato's thought, is a miniature version of the city-state in whom the virtues of justice, courage, wisdom, and moderation should also be present. Plato anticipates Aristotle's view that there are four essential virtues, and Plato, like Aristotle, emphasizes the vital role of wisdom in ordering the city-state and one's own soul. Because wisdom directs both the city as a whole and the individual person, wisdom gives a unity to both the ideal society and the virtues.

Academic Influences

Although Aristotle developed his own philosophical approach, including terminology, method, and division of disciplines, the influence of Plato and his school on Aristotle's work can hardly be overstated. Plato had founded the Academy, the first school for theoretical research in the Western world,* and some of the most talented researchers of the period were associated with it. Following Socrates' example, Plato often analyzed and criticized the most common views of his day—views put forward in his dialogues as the opinions of the Sophists. Aristotle studied and taught at the Academy until Plato's death, for a period of some 20 years, and consequently, he should be viewed as sharing the approach of Socrates and Plato, especially in *Nicomachean Ethics* and *Politics*. The historian of philosophy Terence Irwin* confirms this fact: "Aristotle places himself in the Socratic tradition by endorsing the critical examination of common moral beliefs in order to identify the puzzles and difficulties they raise. In Plato's early dialogues Socrates raises these puzzles through systematic cross-examination of ordinary beliefs."[3]

This is, of course, compatible with the fact that Aristotle would develop distinctive and divergent views later in his career. After such development, Aristotle critically discusses theories of other members or associates of the Academy in *Nicomachean Ethics*, notably those of Plato and the astronomer and mathematician

Eudoxus* and the philosopher Speusippus,* Plato's nephew. Thus, in arriving at his own view, which tends to differ considerably from those of his intellectual mentors and peers, Aristotle often engages fruitfully with his ex-colleagues from the Academy. He also cites examples or quotations from the Pre-Socratics, Plato, Socrates, and the Sophists, as well as from poets and playwrights of the day.

---

1. Alexander Mourelatos (ed.), *The Pre-Socratics: A Collection of Critical Essays* (Princeton, NJ: Princeton University Press, 1993).
2. Anthony Preus, *Historical Dictionary of Ancient Greek Philosophy* (Lanham, MD: Scarecrow Press, 2007), 108.
3. T. Irwin, *The Development of Ethics*, vol. 1 (Oxford: Oxford University Press, 2007), 2.

MODULE 3
THE PROBLEM

KEY POINTS

- Ancient moral philosophers* sought to answer the question "What is happiness?"
- In Aristotle's time it was considered that ordinary people often identified happiness with money or pleasure; politicians identified it with honor; and many philosophers* argued that happiness was a state of the soul.
- Aristotle disagrees with the argument that happiness is a state of the soul; for him, it is activity in accordance with moral and intellectual virtues.*

Core Question

Aristotle begins *Nicomachean Ethics* by asserting, "Every skill and every inquiry, and similarly every action and rational choice, is thought to aim at some good; and so the good has been aptly described as that at which everything aims."[1] Aristotle thus sets up the work's key question with directness and clarity: What is the highest or best good for human beings?

Aristotle assumes that human beings must be aiming at *something* in their actions, and the thing at which all their actions ultimately aim must be consistent with their nature. Two things that guide Aristotle's answer to the question of happiness are reputable opinions (*endoxa*)* and what one can perceive (*phainomena*).* As a general approach in his philosophy, he seeks agreement between reputable previous opinions and daily personal experience.²

Aristotle acknowledges in *Nicomachean Ethics* I.4–5 that there is general agreement that the highest good at which humans aim is *eudaimonia*: * happiness or flourishing. Here it must be noted that in the ancient world, people conceived of happiness as an objective state of being rather than merely a subjective experience. In this, all ancient theories differ from our modern use of "happiness"—that is, it is a state of being independent of our perception, not something that we define for ourselves by feeling it. Although Aristotle agrees with Plato and the ordinary person that happiness is the ultimate good and must be objective, he also sees that there is wide disagreement about what this happiness consists of. As he acknowledges, "They disagree about substantive conceptions of happiness, the masses giving an account which differs from that of the philosophers."³

Aristotle inherits practical disagreement about what is the ultimate good, and he develops a genuinely new idea about the nature of this highest good. He argues that happiness is *an activity*, not a state of being. It is "activity of the soul in accordance with virtue" in a complete life.⁴

> "Most people, I should think, agree about what [the ultimate good] is called, since both the masses and sophisticated people call it happiness, understanding being happy as equivalent with living well and acting well. They disagree about substantive conceptions of happiness."
>
> —— Aristotle, *Nicomachean Ethics*

The Participants

In his dialogues *Republic* and *Philebus*,* Plato suggests that the soul's possession of the virtues is sufficient for happiness (*eudaimonia*). Plato primarily considers the human good as a state of being rather than an activity. For Plato, virtues are character traits possessed within the soul of the individual that can never be taken away by external circumstances. The virtuous person is virtuous, whether or not she or he has an opportunity to express those virtues. Furthermore, Socrates and Plato likened virtue or moral excellence to a craft. It does not matter whether the craftsman enjoys his work or not: as long as the product is good, he has worked well.

Plato argues in *Republic* that strict education for children is necessary if they are to arrive at the virtuous character that creates happiness: since the pull of pleasure and the fear of pain are undeniable for children and young people, they need external authorities such as teachers and parents guiding their behavior and teaching them about the virtues.[5] Finally, the common person's opinion was that happiness consisted of some external good—such as wealth or fame or pleasure—rather than virtue itself.

The Contemporary Debate

In *Nicomachean Ethics* Aristotle begins by considering "reputable" ("*endoxa*") opinions.[6] He advances his own theory only after a detailed and careful analysis of the theories of others, who include philosophers, sages, and poets. Although it is clear that Plato and his teacher Socrates influenced Aristotle the most, the key themes seem to be developed with Plato's view in mind. But Aristotle also paid attention to the ordinary person's opinions about happiness.

Regarding the nature of happiness (*eudaimonia*), Aristotle agrees with Plato that the best life centers on the virtues but there are important differences between their accounts. Aristotle argues, contrary to Plato, that virtue is necessary, but not sufficient, for *eudaimonia*; it is absurd to argue that the person who is internally virtuous but desperately poor is really happy. Instead, Aristotle draws on the popular insight that there is something important for happiness in wealth and honor, arguing that virtuous *action* and contemplation represent the fullest life of happiness, and admitting that some level of money and health is necessary to achieve this.

Aristotle also develops Plato's understanding of the relationship between virtue and pleasure. In *Nicomachean Ethics*, Aristotle follows Plato in acknowledging that pleasure cannot be the ultimate good, stating that "pleasure is not the good, because the good cannot become more worthy of choice by anything's being added to it."[7] According to both Plato and Aristotle, the life of pure pleasure can be improved by also being characterized by reason—in which case pleasure cannot be *the ultimate good*, since the ultimate good must be incapable of being improved on. Aristotle, however, argues that the full development of virtue will mean that the virtuous person takes pleasure in his virtuous activity, so that doing what is right grudgingly indicates that one is not completely virtuous[8]—a slight adjustment of Plato's position.

There is a final important difference between Plato and

Aristotle in regard to ethics.* For Plato, every human action was aimed at the "Form of the Good." This was, for Plato, an abstract concept that united all the things we call "good": a good man, a good intellect, good archery, for example. Though acknowledging that this account has some appeal, Aristotle ultimately disagrees with it, stating that there is no form that all good things (listing the examples of "honor, practical wisdom and pleasure") can meaningfully be said to share.[9] Ethics, therefore, does not require theoretical knowledge of the abstract Form of the Good but only practical wisdom.

---

1. Aristotle, *Nicomachean Ethics*, trans. Roger Crisp (Cambridge: Cambridge University Press, 2014), I.1.1094a,1–3.
2. Aristotle, *Nicomachean Ethics*, VII.I.1145b2–7; cf. Christopher Shields, "Aristotle," *Stanford Encyclopedia of Philosophy*, ed. Edward N. Zalta (Fall 2015 edn.), accessed January 19, 2016, http://plato.stanford.edu/archives/ fall2015/entries/aristotle/.
3. Aristotle, *Nicomachean Ethics*, I.4.1095a16–22.
4. Aristotle, *Nicomachean Ethics*, I.7.1098a16–18.
5. Aristotle, *Nicomachean Ethics*, X.9.1179b16–18 and II.3.1104b12–13.
6. Aristotle, *Nicomachean Ethics*, I.4–5 for some remarks on the method and the assessment of *endoxa*.
7. Aristotle, *Nicomachean Ethics*, 1172b28 ff; Plato, *Philebus*, 60c–61a.
8. Aristotle, *Nicomachean Ethics*, II.3.1104b3–11.
9. Aristotle, *Nicomachean Ethics*, I.6.1096b24; the full argument is found in I.6.1096b10–35.

MODULE 4
THE AUTHOR'S CONTRIBUTION

KEY POINTS

* In *Nicomachean Ethics*, Aristotle considers whether happiness is the highest good of human life, and if so, what is necessary to achieve happiness.
* Aristotle argues that virtue* is necessary, but not sufficient, for happiness; for him, happiness requires virtuous activity, not simply a virtuous state of the soul.
* He draws this insight from combining the ethical theories of the philosopher* Plato* with the beliefs of the common people.

Author's Aims

Aristotle's aim in *Nicomachean Ethics* was to find the highest good of human life,[1] so as to provide both individuals and politicians with a goal and a model of action.[2] It was conventional wisdom that happiness or well-being (*eudaimonia*)* was the thing that every human being aimed at. For Aristotle and other Classical philosophers, *eudaimonia* describes a set of objective facts about the person, rather than merely a passing feeling or opinion of one's life. Some held that happiness is found in wealth, while others located it in honor, and still others in power. However, Aristotle's philosophical predecessors, Plato and Socrates,* had argued that happiness resides in the possession of virtue. Aristotle's inventive approach is to seek to blend these seemingly incompatible conceptions of happiness.

He does so by emphasizing that human good is found in the

exercise of the virtues, stating that the ultimate good is "activity of the soul in accordance with virtue, and if there are several virtues, in accordance with the best and most complete."³ But while the possession of a virtue or the virtues is necessary for happiness, it is not sufficient. One must also possess the external things (such as friendship, financial resources, and so on) that are necessary to act in a virtuous manner. Without these, one's virtuous character does not have the chance to be expressed. For instance, if a person aims at practicing the virtue of generosity but possesses only enough money to buy personal food and shelter, then they will not be able to act with that virtue. The stress on virtuous *activity* reveals Aristotle's originality. Therefore, it is wrong to characterize Aristotle's approach as focused on good character as opposed to right action: Aristotle argues that both are necessary for happiness.

The above sheds some light on Aristotle's "virtue ethics"* (his approach to an ethical theory that maintains that the morality of an action should be judged by the character or virtue of the person, rather than by the outcome of the action).

> "If ... we take the characteristic activity of a human being to be a certain kind of life; and if we take this kind of life to be activity of the soul and actions in accordance with reason ... and a characteristic activity to be accomplished well when it is accomplished in accordance with the appropriate virtue; then if this is so, the human good turns out to be activity of the soul in accordance with virtue, and if there are several virtues, in accordance with the best and most complete."
> ——Aristotle, *Nicomachean Ethics*

Approach

Aristotle's approach to ethics* in *Nicomachean Ethics* is groundbreaking in two ways: in his practical focus, and in his belief that ethical reflection requires ethical education.

Aristotle also develops a more practical approach to ethics than that of his teacher Plato. Aristotle saw that, since human action and society are full of unforeseen events and luck, we cannot approach ethics as an abstract subject. Ethics is practical. So, whereas Plato had suggested a single term covering theoretical and practical wisdom (Greek: *sophia*),* Aristotle divides the intellect into theoretical wisdom (*sophia*), practical wisdom (*phronesis*),* and productive wisdom (skill in producing things). So one need not be a philosopher or theoretically minded to possess virtues such as justice, courage, or temperance.*[4]

Furthermore, Aristotle's approach to ethics differs both from that of his predecessor Plato and from most modern approaches to the subject in not beginning with a theoretical defense of ethical concepts. We might assume, for instance, that Aristotle would begin with an account not only of why happiness consists of virtuous activity, but also of why the traditional characteristics (justice, temperance, courage) count as virtues at all. Such an account would demonstrate to everyone why they should be just and temperate. Indeed, in *Republic*, Plato uses reason to seek a description of virtues such as justice.[5]

Seeking to understand why Aristotle does not address this question, we should consider that, for Aristotle, knowledge of what is and what is not a virtue is decided in the early stages of one's development. As he states several times, a person can be ruined for life with regard to virtue if he or she is not taught early to exercise discipline in pursuing his or her desires; "anyone," he states, "who is going to be a competent student in the spheres of what is noble and what is just … must be brought up well in his habits."[6] While we can later reflect on and refine our understanding of the virtues, we must learn early on to see their essential nature and that they are ultimately worth pursuing.

Contribution in Context

The main argument of *Nicomachean Ethics* concerns the ultimate human good. This good is agreed to consist of happiness, and Aristotle will conclude that happiness is virtuous, rational activity.[7] But he acknowledges the role of the debate in contemporary Athenian philosophy about the nature of happiness; his response to this debate can be viewed as both a critique and a combining of the prevailing opinions about happiness. Aristotle critiques the views of the common people, who think happiness consists of the possession of "pleasure, wealth, or honor."[8] He argues that such things are only ever pursued for the sake of something else. Money, for instance, is pursued for what it can buy a person, so it cannot be the thing at which all human actions are aimed.

Second, Aristotle disagrees with his philosophical predecessors, Plato and Socrates, about whether virtuous character is sufficient for happiness. While the possession of virtue is necessary, it simply cannot be that someone who is virtuous but is "terribly ugly, of low birth, or solitary and childless" has achieved *eudaimonia* (happiness or well-being).[9] Aristotle arguably blends the best aspects of the conventional opinions about happiness. Plato and Socrates were correct that a human being needs virtuous character to be happy, and the common person's opinions were correct in that money and honor are part of what makes happiness possible. For Aristotle, the happy person is the person who both *possesses* moral and intellectual virtues and has the external goods necessary to *act* in a virtuous way. Finally, Aristotle agrees with Plato that the life of philosophical contemplation is the highest good that human beings can attain.

---

1. Aristotle, *Nicomachean Ethics*, trans. Roger Crisp (Cambridge: Cambridge University Press, 2014), I.2.1094a21–22; and I.4.1095a15–17.
2. Aristotle, *Nicomachean Ethics*, I.2.1094b11.
3. Aristotle, *Nicomachean Ethics*, I.7.1098a15–16.
4. Aristotle, *Nicomachean Ethics*, VI.3–5.1139b14–1140b30.
5. See, for instance, Plato, *The Republic*, trans. G. M. A. Grube, in *Readings in Ancient Greek Philosophy*, eds. S. Cohen, P. Curd and C. D. C. Reeve (Indianapolis: Hackett, 2005), 336b and following.
6. Aristotle, *Nicomachean Ethics*, I.4.1095b3–5.
7. Aristotle, *Nicomachean Ethics*, I.7, especially 1098a16–17.
8. Aristotle, *Nicomachean Ethics*, I.4.1095a23–24.
9. Aristotle, *Nicomachean Ethics*, I.8.1099a31–1099b1–5.

SECTION 2
IDEAS

MODULE 5
MAIN IDEAS

KEY POINTS

- The key themes of *Nicomachean Ethics* are happiness, excellence/virtue,* and action; they require a detailed analysis of good action and character, responsibility, justice, friendship, and pleasure.
- Happiness consists of virtuous activity; complete virtue requires both the virtues of character (courage, for example) and the virtues of intellect, especially practical wisdom.
- Aristotle argues that practical wisdom (Greek: *phronesis*)* helps us determine a mean* (or middle) between extreme character traits, and that each virtue represents such a mean.

Key Themes

The overarching goal of Aristotle's *Nicomachean Ethics* is to give an account of the ultimate human good. Aristotle will argue that virtuous activity is the highest good, and he employs five main concepts to make his argument. These are:

- Happiness (*eudaimonia*) *
- The function (*ergon*)* of human beings
- The excellences or virtues (*aretê*)*
- Practical wisdom (*phronesis*)
- The doctrine* (teaching) of the mean—the desirable middle ground.

In Book I.7, we learn that the most important human good is happiness (*eudaimonia*). This is an *endoxa**—one of the starting points from which a coherent moral philosophy* must be built.

What does Aristotle understand by "happiness"? It is not merely a subjective emotional state, something we have to define for ourselves as we feel it, as we think of happiness today; rather, it is an objective state—closer to the concept of well-being or human flourishing. Furthermore, happiness or flourishing is determined by the *ergon*—the "characteristic activity" that defines something.

Defining this further, the characteristic activity that all human beings share in common is living in accordance with certain virtues (*aretê*) of thought and action.[1] The virtues of thought have been called "intellectual virtues"; the virtues of action have been called "moral virtues." Finally, each virtue is a mean between at least two corresponding vices.

> "Aristotle's Nicomachean Ethics *is about what is good for human beings. It asks and proposes an answer to the question 'What is the chief or primary good for man?' and looks at the implications of its answer."*
>
> ——Sarah Broadie, "Philosophical Introduction" to Aristotle's *Nicomachean Ethics*

Exploring the Ideas

The goal of *Nicomachean Ethics* is to give an account of the ultimate human good. To give an account of happiness, Aristotle asks what the characteristic activity or *ergon* of a human being is. For Aristotle, it is reason that makes a human being different from rocks, plants, and other animals, so our account of happiness must be based on the fact that people are essentially rational (reason-based) beings. Aristotle argues that the function of a human (and therefore the key to happiness) is acting in accord with the virtues (*aretê*) because virtuous activity is in accord with the rational nature of human beings.

The rational nature of human beings is a combination of practical and theoretical wisdom. Practical wisdom (*phronesis*) is a very important intellectual virtue for Aristotle's system because it makes living virtuously possible. Aristotle writes, "The mark of a man of practical wisdom [is] to be able to deliberate well about what is good and expedient for himself."[2] The practically wise person does this in two ways. First, the person is able to judge the virtuous thing to do (and how to do it) in a certain situation. Second, the presence of practical wisdom helps the virtuous person control appetites or desires that would otherwise lead them away from acting according to the moral virtues. As Aristotle emphasizes, the judgment of actions and the control of appetites through practical wisdom (*phronesis*) involves "feelings and actions" that are appropriate in certain circumstances.[3]

One may ask why practical wisdom demands action in accord with the virtues. Aristotle suggests that practical wisdom helps us determine which character traits represent the mean between extremes of character. So, for instance, practical wisdom will show us that courage is a mean between the extremes of foolhardiness and cowardice. Foolhardiness is rushing into dangerous situations without necessity or without proper planning; cowardice is shrinking back from a dangerous situation even when an action is required to help others. So, courage—the mean between these two—is the tendency to act in order to achieve some good even when facing the risk of physical harm. Additionally, practical wisdom will help us see that although there is only one virtue to aim at in each area of human life, there may be many corresponding vices to avoid.

What are the virtues that Aristotle associates with human happiness? Virtues are deeply ingrained character traits of thought and action, which include "moral" virtues such as justice, temperance,* generosity, friendship, and courage, as well as "intellectual" virtues such as intelligence, scientific (or certain) knowledge, and practical wisdom (*phronesis*). These virtues cannot be acquired through instruction alone but only through virtuous habits over a long period of time.

Finally, theoretical reason is another part of what separates human beings from animals. So, a thoroughly happy (or flourishing) human life is one in which the person contemplates* abstract and universal truths. The possibility of a life of philosophical activity is part of what separates us from animals and what makes us similar to the gods.[4]

So, for Aristotle, a flourishing or happy life progresses like this:

- From a young age, a person is educated well on the right kinds of habits
- By practicing these habits, the person eventually develops intellectual and moral virtues
- These intellectual and moral virtues together make the

person practically wise—able to recognize and choose virtuous actions consistently and for the sake of virtue
- Finally, the happy person will have the resources necessary to act virtuously and to contemplate abstract philosophical questions. A person who leads a life of morally and intellectually virtuous activity is truly happy.

Language and Expression

The writing of *Nicomachean Ethics* is notoriously dense, probably because it was written to be given as a series of lectures to specialists in the Lyceum.* So, Aristotle's original audience would have been both well educated in philosophy and morally well educated. Furthermore, Aristotle likely would have expanded on the points he makes in the text, using illustrations and perhaps even visual aids.

The language of *Nicomachean Ethics* has had a significant impact on later moral philosophers. Three words have been very influential. First, Aristotle's use of the Greek word for happiness, *eudaimonia*, has produced a certain way of thinking about ethics.* "Eudaimonistic" ethical theories are those that focus on a rich notion of happiness or human flourishing as the goal of ethics. Another important concept that Aristotle invents is practical wisdom or practical rationality: *phronesis*. Following Aristotle, most ethical theories try to account for the relationship between theoretical and practical rationality. Finally, Aristotle's insistence that some end (Greek: *telos*) is being pursued in human action has helped create the category of teleological* ethics. Teleological ethics is usually focused on discovering or describing the end toward which all human action aims, or should aim.

---

1. Aristotle, *Nicomachean Ethics*, trans. Roger Crisp (Cambridge: Cambridge University Press, 2014), I.13.1103a1–10.
2. Aristotle, *Nicomachean Ethics*, VI.5.1140a25 ff.
3. Aristotle, *Nicomachean Ethics*, II.6.1106b17 ff.
4. See Aristotle, *Nicomachean Ethics*, X.7–8.

MODULE 6
SECONDARY IDEAS

KEY POINTS
- Aristotle gives a new account of why people who know the right thing to do often fail to carry it out.
- Justice and friendship, both virtues* that relate more directly to our social lives, are necessary for real flourishing.
- While allowing that good pleasures are key to a good life, Aristotle argues that pleasure cannot be the ultimate good.

Other Ideas

Some very important secondary themes in Aristotle's *Nicomachean Ethics* are voluntary action and responsibility, pleasure and pain, incontinence* (weakness of will), justice and friendship, and the virtuous person's life as a whole.

Aristotle notes that blame and praise can only be reasonably assigned to people who actually had control over what they did. Some may argue that the person who lacks virtue is too used to nonvirtuous habits to be able to choose the virtuous thing; Aristotle could respond that such a person is responsible for having chosen the actions that began the movement away from a virtuous character and toward a vicious one.

Aristotle also believes that pleasure matters for human actions: "Moral virtue is concerned with pleasures and pains; it is on account of the pleasure that we do bad things, and on account of the pain that we abstain from noble ones."[1] Pleasure tends to lead us toward bad acts and toward a lack of self-control; consequently pleasure is often not a good thing. Pleasure, however, is good when it is connected with virtuous activity itself. If the virtuous person sees the need to commit a courageous act of self-sacrifice, for instance, then that act is pleasant to the virtuous person.

> "Some ideas are at once so good and so convincing that it seems a pity that there is no such thing as a Nobel Prize for philosophy ... One of those bright ideas that we should be grateful to have to this very day is Aristotle's ingenious device of integrating pleasure and pain in ethical thought."
> —— Dorothea Frede,* "Pleasure and Pain in Aristotle's Ethics"

Exploring the Ideas

In relation to his account of pleasure and pain, Aristotle also discusses the problem of a weakness of will (*akrasia*).* The problem is this: if happiness (*eudaimonia*)* is the virtuous activity that all human beings aim at, why do people fail to act virtuously— even those who seem to know what will lead to happiness? Plato* had argued that if someone does not act according to virtue, then they must suffer from a lack of knowledge. It could not be the case, according to Plato, that one could know that taking someone's property was unjust and yet still choose to take that person's property. Aristotle, however, seeks to explain the obvious truth that people often seem to know what is right and yet fail to do it; his argument is that the problem lies in the fact that such people are "incontinent"—a term he uses to describe people who lack self-restraint. Weakness of will is, for Aristotle, like a perpetual state of being "asleep, mad, or drunk."[2]

To use a modern example, although a drunken person may claim to know that that it is wrong to drive a car while drunk, it does not surprise us if the person gets behind the wheel anyway; even though drunken people use the same words as sober people, they do not genuinely understand what they are saying when they mutter, "Driving drunk is wrong." They cannot, then, really be said to *know* that it is wrong.

Similarly, an incontinent person (that is, someone who lacks self-control) is too affected by his or her desires to really know the moral claims that he or she puts forward as true. To overcome incontinence, a person must be taught to habitually choose virtuous acts. Once this person has developed the capacity to choose what is virtuous (and to do so *because* it is virtuous), the person is no longer incontinent but is virtuous.

To understand Aristotle's account of happiness, it is important to understand that his virtues were not overly individualistic or inward looking. He sees the task of moral philosophy* as continuous with political concerns. Justice and friendship are therefore important goods in Aristotle's ethical system, in that a flourishing human life will always include them. Aristotle discusses the virtue of justice in Book V and the good of friendship in Books VIII and IX. He identifies two aspects of justice—one that could be called political, and one that could be called personal. Political justice is a state of affairs that achieves the mean*—the desired middle—between one person possessing too much wealth and another person possessing too little wealth.[3]

The personal aspect of justice is a personal virtue of giving people what they deserve, and it is a mean between corresponding vices. Lawless, greedy and unfair people miss the mean and are therefore unjust.[4]

Friendship, for Aristotle, comes in three kinds: friendships of utility (convenience), friendships of pleasure, and friendships of virtue.[5] While the first two are common and sometimes necessary versions of friendship, it is the last of these that is true and lasting: "Complete friendship is that of good people, those who are alike in their virtue."[6] An intriguing characteristic of Aristotle's account of justice and friendship is that, both in *Nicomachean Ethics* and in *Politics*, he suggests that the state (Greek: *polis*)* ought to play a role in developing people's character so that they come to possess the virtue of justice.

Finally, Aristotle's account of the virtues is that *eudaimonia* (happiness) really only applies to life as a whole. He does not think that a person can be said to be virtuous because of just one of his actions; on the contrary, the virtuous person can only truly be judged at the end of life, and he will possess a whole life of virtuous activity, which constitutes happiness. Aristotle states that virtue is truly present "in a complete life. For one swallow does not make a summer, nor does one day."[7] In other words, one instance of a person's fair business dealing does not make it reasonable for us to call that person just.

Overlooked

Although *Nicomachean Ethics* is one of the most highly studied philosophical texts in history, there are still some aspects that have been neglected. One area of relative neglect is the fact that Aristotle sees the great-souled person (that is, one who exhibits *megalopsuchia*)* as the highest example of virtue. A great-souled person is one who takes pride in his own generosity, who believes he is deserving of honor on a grand scale, and who is very much conscious of his own virtue and moral superiority to others. Aristotle viewed this great-souled disposition as a "sort of crown of the virtues."[8] While this account of great-souledness as the achievement of the virtues does not match the modern conception of a virtuous person, it is an important aspect of Aristotle's *Nicomachean Ethics*.

Another relatively neglected aspect of Aristotle's moral system concerns his views on the life of contemplation,* or reflection on eternal truths, and its relationship to the divine. In Book X, Aristotle returns to the question of the highest good. He argues that although action in accordance with *ethical* excellence will result in a happy life, there is something even more complete: the life of philosophical reflection. "If happiness is activity in accordance with virtue," he argues, "it is reasonable that it should be in accordance with the highest virtue ... this activity is contemplative."[9]

Aristotle's concept of a human being, then, is founded on the idea that we are essentially rational. Thus, the philosopher who contemplates mathematical and metaphysical* truths (truths about ultimate reality), as well as truths about God,[10] is said to have achieved the highest happiness and to most resemble God.

1. Aristotle, *Nicomachean Ethics*, trans. Roger Crisp (Cambridge: Cambridge University Press, 2014), II.3.1104b9–10.
2. Aristotle, *Nicomachean Ethics*, VII.3.1147a14.
3. Aristotle, *Nicomachean Ethics*, 1133b32 ff.
4. Aristotle, *Nicomachean Ethics*, V.1.1129a32 ff.
5. Aristotle, *Nicomachean Ethics*, VIII.3.1156a6–1156b35.
6. Aristotle, *Nicomachean Ethics*, VIII.3.1156b8.
7. Aristotle, *Nicomachean Ethics*, I.7.1098a16–17.
8. Aristotle, *Nicomachean Ethics*, IV.3.1124a2.
9. J. M. Cooper, "Contemplation and Happiness: A Reconsideration," in *Reason and Emotion: Essays on Ancient Moral Psychology and Ethical Theory* (Princeton, NJ: Princeton University Press, 1999), *212*–36.
10. Aristotle, *Eudemian Ethics*, eds. Brad Inwood and Raphael Woolf (Cambridge: Cambridge University Press, 2013), 1249b15–25.

MODULE 7
ACHIEVEMENT

KEY POINTS

* Aristotle provides a complete and clear system of the ethical life, centered on human happiness.
* Aristotle's conception of human nature is crucial to developing his account of the virtues* that are central to happiness.
* Although the particular virtues that Aristotle identifies are derived from considering human nature, they also show a cultural influence.

Assessing The Argument

The central aim of Aristotle's *Nicomachean Ethics* is to define what a good life is. In so doing, he clarifies the notions of happiness, excellence/virtue, practical wisdom, pleasure, and friendship. He delivers a complex and detailed anthropology* (a word used here in the sense of a set of beliefs about what humans are) that has contributed to the text's enduring success. Compared with other forms of moral philosophy* of the period, *Nicomachean Ethics* stands out for its systematic and comprehensive structure and for its attempt to account for the variety of human passions and desires from a single perspective. Aristotle makes persuasive arguments against conceiving of happiness as identical to wealth, fame, or power. Similarly, he argues that because virtuous people who suffered torture had a less than happy life, virtuous character alone could not be identical to happiness. The happy person must possess virtues as well as some external goods—such as friendship and pleasure.

Aristotle also improved upon Plato's* suggestion that a person who chooses to do wrong always does so out of a lack of knowledge. Aristotle uses the concept of incontinence (here meaning weakness of will) to demonstrate that although people may have intellectual knowledge of what is right, they still may not do the right thing because of their untrained desires and passions. Aristotle's distinctive emphasis on virtuous *activity*, however, raises this question: If we are to imitate the character of the virtuous in our actions, how do we determine which people are virtuous to begin with?

Some philosophers have pointed out that if virtuous people are meant to show us which actions are right, then it seems circular (that is, a fallacy of reasoning) for Aristotle to say that we know which people are virtuous because of their right actions.

> "Aristotle currently occupies a privileged position in the study of moral philosophy ... [He] is regarded as someone whose approach to the philosophical study of ethics must be learned (though not necessarily accepted) by any serious student of the subject. More than any other philosopher from antiquity ... he is read as someone whose framework for ethics might still be viable."
> —— Richard Kraut, Introduction to *The Blackwell Guide to Aristotle's Nicomachean Ethics*

Achievement in Context

It is very difficult to determine the immediate impact of a text as ancient as *Nicomachean Ethics*, partly because there are virtually no direct quotations of *Nicomachean Ethics* outside of Aristotle's own philosophical school dating from 323 B.C.E. to 45 B.C.E.[1] By the first century B.C.E., Aristotle's ethical views seem to have been eclipsed in popularity by Stoic* ethics and Epicurean* ethics. Followers of the Stoic school of ethics famously held the view, proposed by the philosopher Socrates,* that virtue is sufficient for happiness—and not merely necessary for happiness, as Aristotle had argued; followers of the Epicurean school of ethics, on the other hand, equated happiness with pleasure. It should be noted, however, that it has been argued that *Nicomachean Ethics* did have significant influence on both Stoic and Epicurean ethics.[2]

Social and political forces played an important role in the reception of Aristotle's *Nicomachean Ethics*. For instance, before Aristotle's death in 322 B.C.E., he designated one of his followers, Theophrastus,* as his successor, and some ancient texts report that when Theophrastus in turn died in about 287 B.C.E., Aristotle's writings were taken from the students at his Lyceum* because of a condition in Theophrastus's will.[3] Aristotle's *Nicomachean Ethics*, with his other scholarly works, was not recovered until the Romans captured Athens in around 86 B.C.E.; some of his other works were unavailable in Europe until the twelfth century C.E.

Nicomachean Ethics, once recovered, played a crucial role in the development of the ethical outlook of the late Middle Ages* (the period from about the twelfth to the fifteenth centuries C.E.). For instance, in the thirteenth century, Thomas Aquinas,* the influential medieval* scholar of Christian thought, sought to integrate Aristotle's ethics with the teachings of Christian scripture.

Aquinas integrated Aristotle's account of the role of the virtues of prudence, courage, justice, and practical wisdom, and also restated the supremacy of the contemplative* life, arguing that Aristotle had urged human beings to pursue a life spent contemplating God.[4]

Limitations

- Three philosophical aspects of *Nicomachean Ethics* have caused limitations in its reception—namely:
    - Aristotle's argument relating to the *ergon**—function—of human beings
    - His method of determining the virtues
    - His culturally determined list of the virtues themselves.

The first, and most important, of these is Aristotle's notion of the objective function (*ergon*) of human beings. By this, he meant a function or purpose that exists for all people, even if they do not know it. Aristotle based his ethical system on the idea that an objective function could be discovered in human nature, thereby providing the key to human flourishing (*eudaimonia*).* This function was virtuous activity performed in accord with reason.*

The idea of human beings having a built-in function may have been readily accepted in Aristotle's Athens, but it has often been rejected by those who hold more modern, scientific world views. Indeed, one of the main objections to Aristotle's ethics also applies to his scientific thought. Aristotle had argued that things in nature have purposive (or final) causes* as well as physical causes; he argued, that is, that it is possible not only to know the physical *cause* of a change in nature, but also nature's *purpose*, or goal, in making the change. However, since the scientific revolution of the seventeenth century, science has largely restricted itself to the study of physical causes. In this light, Aristotle's views about both the function of biological* things and the function of human beings are often regarded as unscientific.

Second, many philosophers have asked how Aristotle's account can help the individual determine what to do in a certain situation. Aristotle suggests that practical wisdom (*phronesis*)* will help us know whether a certain action counts as just or unjust, courageous or cowardly. But it is only the person who already possesses the virtues to a significant extent who can be said to be practically wise. The problem here is that before one can know which virtues one ought to aim to develop, one would have to have already developed those virtues. Some philosophers have argued that this is a problematically circular argument.[5]

Finally, although Aristotle means for his list of virtues to apply to all human beings, his account turns on his specific understanding of human nature[6]—and today it is accepted that different cultures hold fundamentally different ideas of virtue.[7]

While Aristotle claims that he provides an exhaustive list of virtues,[8] his list does not contain some virtues that subsequent generations have come to value; it does not include, for example, what came to be important virtues for Christians, such as chastity or humility, nor does it contain the modern virtue of being environmentally conscious.[9] So some of the ethical substance of Aristotle's *Nicomachean Ethics* may be relevant only to a certain time and a certain group of people.

1. Karen M. Nielsen, "The *Nicomachean Ethics* in Hellenistic Philosophy—A Hidden Treasure?" in *The Reception of Aristotle's Ethics*, ed. Jon Miller (Cambridge: Cambridge University Press, 2012), 5.
2. Nielsen, "*Nicomachean Ethics* in Hellenistic Philosophy," 5–7, 19–30.
3. Nielsen, "*Nicomachean Ethics* in Hellenistic Philosophy," 12.
4. Ralph McInerny and John O'Callaghan, "Saint Thomas Aquinas," in *Stanford Encyclopedia of Philosophy*, ed. Edward N. Zalta, (May 23, 2014 edn.), accessed December 10, 2015, http://plato.stanford.edu/entries/ aquinas/#ThoAri.
5. See, for instance, J. L. Mackie, *Ethics: Inventing Right and Wrong* (London: Penguin, 1977), 186.
6. Aristotle, *Nicomachean Ethics*, trans. David Ross, in The Complete Works of Aristotle, ed. J. Barnes (Princeton, NJ: Princeton University Press, 1991), I.7.1097b22–1098a20.
7. The excellences of character—which we could call "moral virtues"—are discussed in Aristotle, *Nicomachean Ethics*, III.6–V.11.
8. Aristotle, *Nicomachean Ethics*, III.6.1115a5 and IV.7.1127a16–17.
9. Rosalind Hursthouse, "Virtue Ethics," section 2, in *Stanford Encyclopedia of Philosophy*, ed. Edward N. Zalta, (Fall 2013 edn.), accessed February 27, 2016, http://plato.stanford.edu/archives/fall2013/entries/ethics-virtue/.

MODULE 8
PLACE IN THE AUTHOR'S WORK

KEY POINTS

- Aristotle wrote on the philosophical* aspects of almost everything there was to know in his time (natural science, psychology, mathematics, rhetoric,* politics), and even invented new sciences such as logic* and biology.*
- Based on an earlier lecture course on ethics,* *Nicomachean Ethics* is a mature work that relies on many of Aristotle's other works.
- The product of extensive research, *Nicomachean Ethics* is one of Aristotle's greatest works; it continues to be seen as a high point in the Aristotelian corpus* (body of work).

Positioning

Aristotle most likely wrote *Nicomachean Ethics* during his most productive time, his second stay in Athens, from 335 to 323 B.C.E., the period in which he composed the majority of his works. Most of the works handed down to us from this period are written roughly, in the form of lecture notes or seminar papers for his school, the Lyceum.* *Nicomachean Ethics* is not the only ethical treatise under Aristotle's name. He also wrote the earlier *Eudemian Ethics* (probably named after one of his students). *Magna Moralia* has also been attributed to Aristotle, but most scholars believe that while this text has key Aristotelian ideas, he probably did not draft it himself.[1]

The relationship between *Nicomachean* and *Eudemian Ethics* is hard to determine—an issue complicated by the fact that the two works share about a third of their content. One modern Aristotle scholar from the United States, Chris Bobonich,* argues, "The more common scholarly opinion is that *Nicomachean Ethics* is the later work, and it has been regarded as Aristotle's major and definitive work on ethics at least since the first or second century [B.C.E.]."[2] Most interpreters agree that *Nicomachean Ethics* is more important than *Eudemian Ethics*, and it is viewed by scholars as the culmination of Aristotle's thinking on moral matters. This is shown by the fact that it draws on almost every other part of his philosophy, such as logic, his thoughts on the human soul, metaphysics* (the branch of philosophy dealing with fundamental questions such as what exists and what is the nature of reality), and his political philosophy. *Politics* starts at the end of *Nicomachean Ethics*, at the end of the tenth book, and the two works are conceived of as a unitary whole.

> "The Corpus of Aristotle's works contains two treatises bearing the name Ethics—the Nicomachean and the Eudemian ... The [Nicomachean] should probably be assigned to the latest period of Aristotle's life, the period of his headship of the Lyceum, i.e. to his fifties or sixties."
> —— David Ross, *The Nicomachean Ethics of Aristotle*

Integration

Aristotle's output as a writer is impressive: ancient catalogues credit him with the authorship of more than 150 books.[3] Many of these works, in particular the popular dialogues, are lost. Only about 2,450 pages in English translation have survived from antiquity. Moreover, Aristotle's body of work was edited to its present state by Andronicus of Rhodes,* a scholar who was probably the leader of the Lyceum in the first century B.C.E. It was Andronicus who originated the famous philosophical word "metaphysics" (literally "after physics") because he placed Aristotle's book by that name after his book on physics. The surviving texts tend to have an unfinished feel, which leads scholars to think they are either lecture notes that Aristotle revised and rewrote over time or notes taken by one of his students during lectures.

Since ancient times, the corpus has been divided into five distinct areas, according to content rather than the order in which they were written. These are:

- Works dealing with logic, known as the *Organon* (the "instrument"), a highly influential set of texts used through the Middle Ages* to teach logic and debate
- Aristotle's landmark works on nature and biology
- *Metaphysics,* an investigation concerning the ultimate nature of reality
- The study of human action, including the two treatises* on ethics—*Nicomachean Ethics* and *Eudemian Ethics*—as well as *Politics*
- A work on the theory of tragedy and the famous *Rhetoric*.[4]

The most important connection between Aristotle's ethical

and political works and his other works is arguably the relationship they bear to his biological theories. While Aristotle spent much time detailing and categorizing species, he also seems to have thought that biological species had certain functions or purposes—an attitude paralleled in Aristotle's understanding of human nature. For Aristotle, there was a certain set of functions that set human beings apart from other animals and thereby gave insight into how we ought to act and live.

Significance

The importance of *Nicomachean Ethics* and of Aristotle's body of work in general is difficult to overestimate. The American professor Ron Polansky* writes, "Aristotle's *Nicomachean Ethics* is among the first systematic treatments of ethics, and it is arguably the most important and influential philosophical work ever devoted to its field. With glorious preparation in the thought of Socrates* and Plato,* and equipped with a rigorous depth in all the principal areas of inquiry, Aristotle aimed for a comprehensive presentation of ethics that could stand the test of time."[5]

The many who follow his philosophy more closely are called Aristotelians, or Peripatetics,* after the circular walkway (*peripatos*) that stood next to the Lyceum.

The philosophy of Aristotle was extremely influential during the late Middle Ages (around 1200–1500 c.e.). During this time, Aristotle was simply called "The Philosopher," and his works represented the most highly regarded wisdom about the world. Great thinkers, such as the Italian astronomer Galileo

Galilei,* the French philosopher René Descartes,* and the Polish astronomer Nicolaus Copernicus,* started to move away from Aristotle's theories about nature in the sixteenth and seventeenth centuries, especially in physics and astronomy. Additionally, moral philosophers,* such as David Hume* and Immanuel Kant,* moved away from Aristotle in the eighteenth century. Despite this historical change, *Nicomachean Ethics* maintained its importance as a classic in moral philosophy.

There is a vast literature on Aristotle, and on *Nicomachean Ethics* in particular. The work has also played a significant role in contemporary moral philosophy. The recent "virtue ethics"* movement, which focuses on moral character as the basis for ethics, is inspired by Aristotle's emphasis on virtue in moral conduct. Famous modern moral philosophers, such as the English virtue ethicist Philippa Foot,* the Scottish thinker Alasdair MacIntyre,* and the US scholar Martha Nussbaum,* are followers of Aristotle.[6]

---

1. For an argument in favor of the authenticity of the *Magna Moralia* see J. M. Cooper, "The *Magna Moralia* and Aristotle's Moral Philosophy," *American Journal of Philology* (1973): 327–49. Against it argues C. Rowe, "A Reply to John Cooper on the *Magna Moralia*," *American Journal of Philology* (1975): 160–72.
2. Aristotle, *Nicomachean Ethics*, trans. David Ross, in *The Complete Works of Aristotle*, ed. J. Barnes (Princeton, NJ: Princeton University Press, 1991), viii; and Chris Bobonich, "Aristotle's Ethical Treatises," in *The Blackwell Guide to Aristotle's Nicomachean Ethics*, ed. Richard Kraut (London: Wiley–Blackwell, 2006), 12–36. The most trenchant critique of the standard view is offered by Anthony Kenny, *The Aristotelian Ethics: A Study of the Relationship Between the* Eudemian *and* Nicomachean Ethics *of Aristotle* (Oxford: *Clarendon Press,* 1978).
3. Diogenes Laertius V.21 ff., in Diogenes Laertius, *Lives of Eminent Philosophers*, ed. R. D. Hicks

(Cambridge, MA: *Harvard University Press,* 1966).
4. All works are found in Barnes, *Complete Works of Aristotle*.
5. R. Polansky, "Introduction: Ethics as Practical Science," in *The Cambridge Companion to Aristotle's Nicomachean Ethics*, ed. R. Polansky (Cambridge: Cambridge University Press, 2014), 1.
6. M. C. Nussbaum, "Non-Relative Virtues: An Aristotelian Approach," in *The Quality of Life*, eds. M. C. Nussbaum and A. Sen (Oxford: Clarendon Press, 1993), 242–69.

SECTION 3
IMPACT

MODULE 9
THE FIRST RESPONSES

KEY POINTS

* It is likely that *Nicomachean Ethics* resulted from the revision of Aristotle's earlier *Eudemian Ethics*.
* It is impossible to form a complete critical history of Aristotle's *Nicomachean Ethics* starting at the time it was written.
* Stoicism,* Epicureanism,* and Skepticism,* approaches to virtuous behavior founded by Aristotle's contemporaries, were the competing moral systems in the centuries after *Nicomachean Ethics* was published.

Criticism

It is not easy to assess the immediate influence, positive or negative, of Aristotle's *Nicomachean Ethics*. Unlike Plato's* influential work on government in *Republic*—which sparked responses from quite a few of its ancient Greek and Roman readers—*Nicomachean Ethics* does not seem to have been published. There is no reference to it in any surviving text until the first century B.C.E., when a reference is found in *De Finibus* (*On Ends*) by Cicero (106–43 B.C.E.). This indicates that it was probably not circulated outside of Aristotle's school, the Lyceum,* during his lifetime or for some time after his death in 322 B.C.E. This would explain why there are no direct criticisms of *Nicomachean Ethics*, and no responses by Aristotle to these criticisms.

Nevertheless, the Aristotelian position was sufficiently well known that it was probably considered, if not by name then at least in spirit, by all the major Hellenistic* schools: the Stoics, the Epicureans, and the Skeptics. (The Hellenistic period—from Hellas, the Greek name for the territory—lasted from the death of Alexander the Great* in 323 B.C.E. to the beginning of the Roman Empire in 31 B.C.E.) The Stoics did not accept Aristotle's view that external goods are necessary for happiness, and instead held to the Socratic* view that virtue is sufficient to achieve happiness. The Epicureans equated happiness with moderate pleasure, rather than with the activity of a rational soul, while the Skeptics disagreed with Aristotle's claim that we can really know what virtue is, claiming that philosophical* reflection will not assist us in discovering or achieving it.

> *"Writing the reception history of the* Nicomachean Ethics *in Hellenistic philosophy is, arguably, an impossible task. The problem is not simply the paucity of evidence. We have no direct citations tying any doctrine discussed by Epicurean, Stoic, or Academic [that is, adherents of the form of skepticism about ethical knowledge which came about in Plato's Academy] philosophers to views explicitly defended by Aristotle in the* [Nicomachean Ethics]*."*
> ——Karen M. Nielsen, *"The Nicomachean Ethics in Hellenistic Philosophy"*

Responses

In the history of moral philosophy,* Professor Terence Irwin* has said that "we can follow one significant thread through the history of moral philosophy by considering how far Aristotle is right, and what his successors think about his claims."[1] Regarding the first responses, however, this assessment is difficult to make since we have little or no direct evidence of the responses to Aristotle's *Nicomachean Ethics* during his lifetime.

We do, however, know that defenders of Aristotle's ethical system existed later in the ancient world. Alexander of Aphrodisias* of the late second and early third century C.E., for example, argues against the Stoics' view that the faultless exercise of virtue is all one could desire. For him, the virtuous person also wants his or her action to achieve its purpose. According to Stoic thought, it does not matter whether the money one gives to charity really reaches the people in need: if one has acted virtuously, and the money is misused through no fault of one's own, then one's action is as good as it could be. Alexander, however, defends what he takes to be Aristotle's view, as Aristotle emphasizes that reaching the goal is important for morally good action.[2] Aristotle did not, then, himself do battle with his critics; instead, his followers fought for him. This is a recurring—and continuing—pattern in the history of Aristotelian philosophy.

Conflict and Consensus

While there is no direct historical evidence of Aristotle receiving criticism of his ethical views and changing them in response, this must largely be on account of the historical distance between Aristotle and readers today. It would surely be wrong to assume that Aristotle did not take criticism at the time into account, and that no critical interaction with his ethical thought took place. On the contrary, since Aristotle was at one point a student at Plato's

Academy* and at another point the head of the philosophical school called the Lyceum, it is likely that he received feedback and criticism of his views over the course of his philosophical career.

Furthermore, most scholars attribute the authorship of two ethical treatises* to Aristotle: *Nicomachean Ethics* and *Eudemian Ethics*.[3] It is significant, however, that although the two works have three books in common (*Nicomachean Ethics* V–VII and *Eudemian Ethics* IV–VI), there are important ethical concepts that differ between the two. For instance, Aristotle's concept of practical wisdom (*phronesis*)* is not consistent over the two works. In *Eudemian Ethics*, it is a more abstract, theoretical faculty (similar to what Plato termed *sophia**—wisdom); in *Nicomachean Ethics*, it is exclusively practical.[4] Since the division of the sciences between theoretical, practical, and productive activities is Aristotle's final position, it would seem that Aristotle wrote *Nicomachean Ethics* after *Eudemian Ethics*—likely after a revision of some of his ethical concepts. Such an account also aligns with the fact that Aristotle increasingly moved away from Plato's philosophical position over the course of his life. This theory is based on the nature of the texts themselves, however, rather than on external evidence.

---

1. T. Irwin, *The Development of Ethics*, Vol. 1 (Oxford: Oxford University Press, 2007), 4.
2. Aristotle, *Nicomachean Ethics*, rev. ed., trans. Roger Crisp (Cambridge: Cambridge University Press, 2014), X.7.1177b16–26.
3. "Introduction" by Roger Crisp, in Aristotle, *Nicomachean Ethics*, vii–viii.
4. Frederick Copleston, *A History of Philosophy: Greece and Rome* (London: Continuum Press, 2003), 270.

MODULE 10
THE EVOLVING DEBATE

KEY POINTS

* Aristotle's systematic exploration of virtue* greatly influenced Christian and non-Christian approaches to virtue.
* Aristotle's philosophy as a whole, including ethics,* was continued after his death by his followers, called the Peripatetics,* and, more critically, by followers of Plato.*
* The medieval* Christian scholar Thomas Aquinas's* interpretation of Aristotle's ethics, which sees human nature as the key for virtue and good action, continues to be explored by neo-Aristotelians*—that is, scholars who draw on Aristotle's ideas—today.

Uses And Problems

Although Aristotle's *Nicomachean Ethics*, completed between 335 and 323 B.C.E., has proved one of the most influential works in the history of philosophy, its popularity and influence have varied over time. During the period immediately after Aristotle's death, the development of his ethics apparently took place primarily within his school, the Lyceum.* The members of this school are known as the Peripatetics. Aristotle's system was eclipsed during the Hellenistic* (322–31 B.C.E.) and Roman* (27 B.C.E.–395 C.E.) periods by Stoic* ethics and Epicureanism*—different approaches to the definition of the well-lived life.

Epicureanism was a school founded by the Greek philosopher Epicurus* (341–270 B.C.E.), who argued that happiness consists of pleasure (Greek: *hedone*).* Epicurus, however, defines pleasure as "freedom from bodily pain and mental anguish," and he believed that virtues (such as justice and temperance)* protect one from the psychological distress caused by indiscriminate pleasure seeking[1]—a view incompatible with that of Aristotle. For Aristotle, virtuous activity *is* happiness, and pleasure coincides with it; for Epicurus, pleasure *is* happiness and virtue is the way to attain pleasure. Though there is no direct evidence for an influence of Aristotle upon Epicureanism, some scholars believe that since the key categories are the same, Aristotle had an influence on Epicureanism.[2]

The Stoics, following Socrates* and Plato, held that virtuous character is sufficient for happiness. While this contradicted Aristotle's theory about happiness, many scholars maintain that Aristotle nonetheless had an impact on Stoic ethical concepts. An example of this influence is the Stoic emphasis on actions "according to nature"—an idea similar to Aristotle's emphasis on determining ethics through the study of human nature.[3] So, it is reasonable to see both Epicureanism and Stoicism as in some ways evolving from Aristotle's ethical categories.

Aristotle's ethics were embraced extensively during the Christian Middle Ages* (the fifth to the fifteenth centuries c.e.), when many philosophers and religious scholars (among them Albertus Magnus* and Thomas Aquinas in the thirteenth century) wrote commentaries on *Nicomachean Ethics*.[4] Later philosophers continued this attention during the Renaissance,* the period of the fourteenth to the seventeenth centuries during which European culture was reinvigorated by a turn toward classical models. The philosopher Francisco Suarez,* for instance, agrees with Aristotle that human nature has universal purposes that form the basis for ethics.

Later philosophers, however, increasingly disagreed with the medieval linkage between Aristotelian and Christian ethics. The British philosopher Thomas Hobbes* (1588–1679 c.e.), for example, argued that physical causes are responsible for all human behavior, rather than final or purposive causes* (that is, the goals or purposes of a person's behavior). Hobbes' view—that human actions resemble the workings of a machine rather than being the result of a person exercising free will—became more dominant in modern philosophy.[5] There was therefore a decline in the popularity of Aristotelian ethics as a complete system in the centuries following the Middle Ages. Around the middle of the twentieth century, however, many philosophers returned to Aristotle as an enlightening moral philosopher for the contemporary world.

> "Aquinas has at least three aims in his moral philosophy: 1) He tries to say what Aristotle means, and what an Aristotelian conception of morality commits us to. 2) He tries to show that this conception of morality is defensible on philosophical grounds. 3) He seeks to show that it also satisfies the theological and moral demands of Christian doctrine."
>
> ——Terence Irwin, *The Development of Ethics*

Schools of Thought

Perhaps the most important school of thought established by

Aristotle's ethics is the medieval Scholastic* tradition. Within this tradition, medieval scholars translated and critically interpreted the writings of Plato, Aristotle, and the Bible. In this process, they sought to combine all these sources of moral and philosophical authority. Such commentaries include the *Super Ethica*—the philosopher Albertus Magnus's commentary on Aristotle's *Nicomachean Ethics*. The book was completed in about 1250 C.E. and became arguably the most influential book on ethics written in the Middle Ages.[6] Also important was Thomas Aquinas's commentary, a work completed in the early 1270s C.E. Most importantly, Aquinas combined Aristotle's ethical system into his extremely influential masterwork, *Summa Theologiae* (written from 1265 to 1274). Aquinas, following Aristotle, maintains that each virtue is a mean* (or desired middle) between vices, and holds that practical reason (in Aquinas's Latin, *prudentia*) is the source of our knowledge concerning which actions and character traits are indeed virtuous.[7]

Indeed, Terence Irwin* argues that Aquinas attempted to build a philosophical defense of Aristotle's ethics and to combine it with Christian thought. Aquinas was respectful of Aristotle, and Irwin describes how he was deeply affected by Aristotle's moral theory. It should be noted here, however, that many scholars argue that Aquinas contributed his own philosophical reflection, which improved upon Aristotle's ethics.[8] Even so, because of the influence that Aquinas's work had upon subsequent Christian theologians, Aristotle can be said to have exercised an influence upon the intellectual and ethical outlook of the Middle Ages.

In Current Scholarship

The past 60 years or so have seen renewed interest in the relevance of Aristotle's ethics to both academic philosophy and the modern world. As evidence of this, recent years have seen two entire anthologies devoted to *Nicomachean Ethics*. These are *The Cambridge Companion to Aristotle's* Nicomachean Ethics, and *Aquinas and the* Nicomachean Ethics.[9] The second work demonstrates Aristotle's influence through other traditions, from the Middle Ages to the twenty-first century. This latest renewal of interest in *Nicomachean Ethics* began with the British philosopher Elizabeth Anscombe's* 1958 article "Modern Moral Philosophy,"[10] which called for a reexamination of Aristotle's ethics in light of moral philosophers' confused use of the notion of "moral obligation" in twentieth-century moral theory. Such an examination, said Anscombe, would push us to seek a clear definition of "a virtue," and might bring with it fresh insights into ethics.

Many moral philosophers have since sought to develop an essentially Aristotelian account of ethics; two of the most prominent are the Scottish philosopher Alasdair MacIntyre* and the philosopher Rosalind Hursthouse* of New Zealand. MacIntyre wrote the highly influential book *After Virtue* (1981), in which he argues that the contemporary world is characterized by incoherence and unending disagreement about ethics, stemming from a modern rejection of Aristotle's belief in the intrinsic purposes of human nature.[11] A more consistent approach, MacIntyre argues, will only be recovered as some form of Aristotle's ethics.

Similarly, Hursthouse argues in her *On Virtue Ethics* (2001) that it is a mistake to think of virtue ethics* as focused only on the character of the individual. Rather, virtue ethics is able to provide concrete guidance about the appropriate norms or principles of behavior. Hursthouse's account provides rules related to virtues and vices. As she states, "Not only does each virtue generate a prescription—do what is honest, charitable, generous—but each vice a prohibition—do not do what is dishonest, uncharitable, mean."[12] Hursthouse follows Aristotle's *Nicomachean Ethics* in both her emphasis on the virtues and her insistence that virtuous *action* is the aim of her theory.

---

1. Quoted from Diogenes Laertius, *Lives of Eminent Philosophers*, ed. R. D. Hicks (Cambridge, MA: Harvard University Press, 1966), X.129–32; also quoted in M. Andrew Holowchak, Happiness and Greek Ethical Thought (London: Continuum Press, 2005), 76.
2. See Karen M. Nielsen, "The *Nicomachean Ethics* in Hellenistic Philosophy: A Hidden Treasure?" in *The Reception of Aristotle's Ethics*, ed. Jon Miller (Cambridge: Cambridge University Press, 2012), 6–8.
3. Nielsen, "*Nicomachean Ethics* in Hellenistic Philosophy," 6; and A. A. Long, "Aristotle's Legacy to Stoic Ethics," *Bulletin of the Institute of Classical Study* 15, no. 1 (1968): 72–85.
4. Anthony Celano, "The Relation of Prudence and *Synderesis* to Happiness in the Medieval Commentaries on Aristotle's Ethics," in Miller, *The Reception of Aristotle's Ethics*, 125–54.
5. See Donald Rutherford, "The End of Ends? Aristotelian Themes in Early Modern Ethics," in Miller, *Reception of Aristotle's Ethics*, 194–221.
6. Celano, "Relation of Prudence and *Synderesis* to Happiness," 138; see also R. A. Gauthier "Trois commentaries 'averroistes' sur l'Ethique a Nicomaque," *Archives d'histoire doctrinale et litteraire du moyen age* 16, no. 1 (1947–8): 187–336.
7. Jennifer A. Herdt, "Aquinas's Aristotelian Defense of Martyr Courage," in *Aquinas and the Nicomachean Ethics*, eds. Tobias Hoffman, Jorn Muller and Matthias Perkams (Cambridge: Cambridge University Press, 2013), 125; cf. John Finnis, "Aquinas's Moral, Political, and Legal

Philosophy," in *Stanford Encyclopedia of Philosophy*, ed. by Edward N. Zalta (Summer 2014 edn.), accessed January 15, 2016, http://plato.stanford.edu/archives/sum2014/ entries/aquinas-moral-political/.

8. For an account of this ethical system, as well as Aquinas's divergences from Aristotle, see Finnis, "Aquinas's Moral, Political, and Legal Philosophy".

9. See R. Polansky (ed.), *The Cambridge Companion to Aristotle's* Nicomachean Ethics (Cambridge: Cambridge University Press, 2014); and Tobias Hoffman, Jörn Muller and Matthias Perkams (eds.), *Aquinas and the* Nicomachean Ethics (Cambridge: Cambridge University Press, 2013).

10. G. E. M. Anscombe, "Modern Moral Philosophy," *Philosophy* 33, no. 124 (1958): 1–19.

11. See Alasdair MacIntyre, *After Virtue*, 3rd edn. (Notre Dame: University of Notre Dame Press, 2007), 1–3, 109–20.

12. Rosalind Hursthouse, *On Virtue Ethics* (Oxford: Oxford University Press, 2001), 36.

MODULE 11
IMPACT AND INFLUENCE TODAY

KEY POINTS

- *Nicomachean Ethics* is a key text for the development of contemporary virtue ethics.*
- Those critical of virtue ethics complain that virtue* does not give you a sufficient set of rules to guide action—it tells you to act well, but not what to do.
- Virtue ethicists deny that an ethical system can specify a straightforward rule for what to do in any given situation, so that practical wisdom (*phronesis*)* is a necessary part of an adequate moral philosophy.*

Position

The ideas put forward in Aristotle's *Nicomachean Ethics* are key to understanding the history of moral philosophy. However, between the beginning of the nineteenth century and the 1950s, Aristotle's approach was not viewed as a practical philosophical option. In 1958, the British philosopher Elizabeth Anscombe* challenged this in a highly influential article on modern moral philosophy.[1] She contrasted modern moral philosophers with Aristotle, arguing that they failed to give a coherent account of the meaning of "moral ought" and "moral obligation."[2] She noted, however, that Aristotle maintained a coherent ethical system without using such problematic terms; rather, Aristotle focused on richer concepts such as "justice" and "courage." So, a return to his ethics could provide a way forward in understanding morality through developing an updated account of the virtues. This text helped launch the neo-Aristotelian* movement—a school of modern thinkers whose work centers on virtue ethics.

In the 1980s, Alasdair MacIntyre's* *After Virtue* (1981) discussed the nature of a virtue; this was an updated version of Aristotle's argument regarding function (*ergon*).* In *After Virtue*, MacIntyre argues that the function of human beings is determined by the nature of the roles they fill in a society, rather than by universal biological purpose, as Aristotle had suggested. According to MacIntyre, the virtues are those well-formed character traits necessary for excellence within different practices and social roles.

Finally, the New Zealand philosopher Rosalind Hursthouse's* *On Virtue Ethics* (2001) sought to revive Aristotle's views on virtues, arguing that they provide guidance on how people should act in certain situations, while vices offer guidance on avoiding certain actions. These examples show that over the past 60 years there has been a revival of Aristotle's ideas.

> *"The particular version of virtue ethics I detail in the book is ... known as 'neo-Aristotelian.' The general kind is 'neo' for at least the reason ... that its proponents allow themselves to regard Aristotle as just plain wrong on slaves and women. ... It is 'Aristotelian' insofar as it aims to stick pretty close to his ethical writings wherever else it can."*
>
> ——Rosalind Hursthouse, *On Virtue Ethics*

Interaction

The current revival of Aristotle's *Nicomachean Ethics* represents a challenge to the major ethical theories of our day—consequentialism* and Kantian* ethics.* Consequentialism states that the goodness of an action or an intention or an emotion is determined by its consequences alone; Kantian ethics states that an action is right if, and only if, it is an expression of a rule that could (with consistency) be made a universal law for all rational beings.[3]

For the first half of the twentieth century, Aristotle's *Nicomachean Ethics* seemed irrelevant in comparison with these two systems of ethics. However, because of Anscombe's highly influential criticisms of modern moral philosophy, Aristotle's work has more recently received greater attention.[4]

The philosophers grouped as neo-Aristotelians have criticized consequentialism and Kantian ethics in several ways.

First, they have pointed out that the development of character is important in moral education and ethical reflection. An approach—such as Aristotle's—that stresses the development of the virtues reflects our actual moral development more than an account that only produces rules for what actions to avoid or carry out.

Second, virtue ethicists have emphasized the important relationship between emotions and the moral life.[5] A rationalistic* approach, such as Kantian ethics, founded on the assumption that knowledge must be derived from theoretical reason, often fails to appreciate how much people rely on their emotions in deciding what is the right action. As Hursthouse argues, "there is indeed much in Kant" to suggest that his account "makes the emotions no part of our rational nature."[6] Her emphasis on combining emotion with practical rationality is a development of Aristotle's view that practical rationality must govern both our feelings *and* our actions; as Aristotle says, "virtue is to do with feelings and actions."[7]

Finally, virtue ethicists argue that other ethical theories, such as consequentialism, rely on problematic ideas of human nature or basic values. For instance, utilitarianism,* a form of consequentialism, relies on the assumption that we should maximize pleasure and reduce pain in all our actions. As Aristotle pointed out, however, "pleasure" is often a confused concept.[8] Sometimes it stands for some psychological state; at other times, it stands for a certain kind of activity.[9] Accordingly, we can speak of pleasure as the positive psychological side effect of something we like or we can say things like "playing soccer is my favorite pleasure." On the basis of Aristotle's insights about the ambiguous ways we talk about pleasure, Anscombe argues that utilitarians "do not notice the difficulty with the concept of pleasure."[10]

This notion of pleasure, then, cannot be the basis for ethics in its entirety. As a result of these arguments from virtue ethicists, many proponents of consequentialist and Kantian ethics have sought to provide an account of the role of the virtues and moral development from within their own systems.[11]

The Continuing Debate

As stated above, Kantianism bases the rightness of actions on whether people are acting according to an appropriate rule, and consequentialism holds that the rightness of an action depends solely on expected outcomes. Supporters of these theories have highlighted several objections to virtue ethics generally and to Aristotle's ethics particularly.

First of all, virtue ethics, especially as Aristotle presents it in *Nicomachean Ethics*, seems to fall short of providing us with actual ethical guidance. Aristotle and his followers maintain that the highest good for human beings is acting in accord with the virtues. But Aristotle also thinks we develop moral character by habits in our early moral education, and without this moral education, we cannot become the kind of people who recognize the goodness of the life of virtue—a person must have good character before he can recognize what it takes to develop the virtues. As the philosopher J. L. Mackie* concludes, "this is too circular to be very helpful."[12]

Some moral philosophers object to Aristotle's ethics because his list of virtues is based on the culture in which he lived, rather than on enduring, universal truth. As the British moral philosopher Bernard Williams* summarizes, "there is a question to be discussed about the extent of the distance we should acknowledge between Aristotle's conceptions and styles of ethical thought and styles of ethical thought we might find acceptable now."[13] Thus, Aristotelians face the task of explaining that while virtues apparently change over time, ethical truth does not.

Most would now argue, for example, that Aristotle's exclusion of women (and all people without property) from the possibility of virtue is a significant cultural blind spot. The moral philosopher Martha Nussbaum* pushes back on the charge that Aristotle simply reflects his culture's values, however, writing, "If we probe further into the way in which Aristotle in fact [numbers and distinguishes] the virtues, we begin to notice things that cast doubt upon the suggestion that he simply described what was admired in his own society."[14] While Aristotle was influenced by his own Athenian context, he sought to both defend its best aspects and criticize what was lacking. So, while one might admit that Aristotle's list of the virtues is not perfect or universal, this is not necessarily a reason to abandon his basic approach to the ethical life. One simply needs to be open to revising one's list of the virtues if someone else has a better list.[15]

---

1. G. E. M. Anscombe, "Modern Moral Philosophy," *Philosophy* 33, no. 124 (1958).
2. Anscombe, "Modern Moral Philosophy," 4–5.
3. For a version of Kantian ethics, see Christine Korsgaard, *Sources of Normativity* (Cambridge: Cambridge University Press, 2012), 19–20.
4. Anscombe, "Modern Moral Philosophy."
5. Aristotle, *Nicomachean Ethics*, trans. Roger Crisp (Cambridge: Cambridge University Press, 2014), I.8.1099a7–21; II.6.1106b16–17.
6. Rosalind Hursthouse, *On Virtue Ethics* (Oxford: Oxford University Press, 2001), 109.
7. Aristotle, *Nicomachean Ethics*, III.1,1109b30; cf. II.5, 1105b20 ff.
8. Aristotle, *Nicomachean Ethics*, X.5, 1175a23 ff.
9. See G. E. M. Anscombe, "Modern Moral Philosophy;" and Alasdair MacIntyre, *After Virtue* (Notre Dame: University of Notre Dame Press, 2007), 62–4.
10. Anscombe, "Modern Moral Philosophy," 2.
11. For an account of the virtues in David Hume and Immanuel Kant's moral philosophies, see Martha Nussbaum, "Virtue Ethics: A Misleading Category?" *Journal of Ethics* 3, no. 3 (1999): 163–201.
12. J. L. Mackie, *Ethics: Inventing Right and Wrong* (London: Penguin, 1977), 186.
13. Bernard Williams, *Ethics and the Limits of Philosophy* (London: Routledge, 2006), 49.
14. Martha Nussbaum, "Non-Relative Virtues: An Aristotelian Approach," *Midwest Studies in Philosophy* 13, no. 1 (1998): 34.
15. For an example of this approach, see Alasdair MacIntyre's *Whose Justice? Which Rationality?* (London: Duckworth, 1988), especially "The Rationality of Traditions," 349–69.

MODULE 12
WHERE NEXT?

KEY POINTS

- *Nicomachean Ethics* will continue to be one of the most influential treatises* on ethics.*
- As the classic text on virtue ethics,* supporters and opponents of virtue ethics will continue to refer to Aristotle's *Nicomachean Ethics*; discussion will continue to return to it.
- *Nicomachean Ethics* provides a comprehensive ethical system of virtue essential to many ethical systems that center on virtue.

Potential

The potential of Aristotle's *Nicomachean Ethics* to influence contemporary and future philosophy* is mainly linked to the fortunes of virtue ethics.[1] Virtue ethicists take their inspiration and key themes from *Nicomachean Ethics*, highlighting topics such as virtue, happiness, and practical wisdom. As Rosalind Hursthouse* writes, "Virtue ethics is both an old and a new approach to ethics, old in so far as it dates back to the writings of Plato* and, more particularly, Aristotle, new in that, as a revival of this ancient approach, it is a fairly recent addition to contemporary moral theory."[2]

There is now sustained philosophical interest in the question of whether virtue ethics really does provide a useful alternative to standard moral theories, and whether Aristotle's version of virtue ethics is the best one.

Furthermore, there is an effort to expand upon Aristotle's

Nicomachean Ethics, making its framework relevant even to issues he did not speak to directly. The Aristotle scholar Sarah Broadie* believes that Aristotelians must be careful in this area. In spite of the fact that "much of what [Aristotle] *does* have to say in *Nicomachean Ethics* continues to shape our own thinking," she writes, we tend to overlook the equally important fact that "many of our own central preoccupations in ethics are with questions on which, for one or another reason, Aristotle has little or nothing to say."[3] In these cases, some virtue ethicists give an answer that they take to be in the Aristotelian spirit. This, in turn, prompts scholars to look at the text afresh, with the concerns of modern virtue ethicists in mind.

> "While it is possible that Aristotle does not, after all, have a virtue ethics, the realization of this possibility is at odds with the expressly neo-Aristotelian character of much virtue ethics, so nicely expressed by Ruth Anna Putnam's ostensive definition of virtue ethics: '... virtue ethics is what Aristotle did.'"
> ——Sean McAleer, "An Aristotelian Account of Virtue Ethics"

Future Directions

The rise of virtue ethics is also responsible for the further development of core aspects of *Nicomachean Ethics*, although not all virtue ethicists are neo-Aristotelians.* Although many virtue ethicists agree with Aristotle's central argument that a good life consists of virtuous activity,[4] some aspects of the text need to be updated, seeming to be tailored for a certain society at a certain time—namely, Athens in the fourth century B.C.E. Thus, Aristotle's virtues are not necessarily our virtues (and vice versa);[5] Aristotle has no virtue that would cover our interaction with the environment, for example. In the future, virtue ethics will continue to provide fruitful discussions of questions about abortion (termination of pregnancy), euthanasia (mercy killing), and medical research from a virtue ethics perspective.[6]

Since virtue plays such an important role in ethical development, educators have begun to focus again more on the development of character. This insight goes back to a concern voiced by Aristotle in the text's final book: that moral education must begin at a young age.[7] Some educators have argued that one should explain to the child the relevant virtue and vice in a given situation, and discourage or encourage the child in terms of virtue and vice.[8] Even if Aristotle does not cover all of our practical concerns, *Nicomachean Ethics* is still relevant, and provides a useful framework within which to develop virtues for our society and time. The Aristotle scholar Paula Gottlieb* remarks, "No doubt in all Aristotle's ethical works there are gems waiting to be discovered and fruitful new lines of enquiry to be pursued, even after two thousand years of study."[9]

Summary

Aristotle's *Nicomachean Ethics* is an ancient, well-organized, highly original, and groundbreaking discussion of ethical theory. Its central argument is that the human good consists of activity—action—in accord with the moral and intellectual virtues. Aristotle ties in almost all of the elements that we still find important in ethical theory: moral character and its acquisition; human action; emotion; pleasure; and the virtues. Hursthouse has summarized the influence of Aristotle's ethics as follows, "Virtue ethics' founding fathers are Plato* and, more particularly, Aristotle ... and it persisted as the dominant approach in Western moral philosophy* until at least the Enlightenment.* It suffered a momentary eclipse during the nineteenth century but re-emerged in the late 1950s in Anglo-American philosophy."[10]

In short, Aristotle's *Nicomachean Ethics* has had a profound impact on the study of philosophy.

The contemporary re-emergence of Aristotle's ethics has had a widespread impact upon moral philosophy, and there are signs that this influence will continue. *Nicomachean Ethics* still has few rivals even among the most influential works of its period dealing with ethics. But this influence is not merely academic. Aristotle's emphasis on the virtues has been implemented in contemporary critiques of the social and economic system of capitalism,*[11] in approaches to environmental care,[12] and in ethical problems in the medical field.[13] Hence *Nicomachean Ethics* remains—and will remain—one of the most important texts in the history of philosophy.

---

1. Important works are collected in R. Crisp and M. A. Slote, (eds.), *Virtue Ethics* (Oxford: Oxford University Press, 1997).

2. Rosalind Hursthouse, *On Virtue Ethics* (Oxford: Oxford University Press, 2001), 9.
3. Sarah Broadie, "Aristotle and Contemporary Ethics," in *The Blackwell Guide to Aristotle's Nicomachean Ethics*, ed. R. Kraut (Oxford: Wiley-Blackwell, 2006), 344.
4. This claim and the argument supporting it are found in Aristotle, *Nicomachean Ethics*, trans. David Ross, in Aristotle, *Nicomachean Ethics*, trans. Roger Crisp (Cambridge: Cambridge University Press, 2014), I.7.1098a7–20.
5. Compare the virtues discussed in Aristotle, *Nicomachean Ethics*, III.6–V.11.
6. Evidence of such a development of virtue ethics is the publication of Michael Austin, *Virtues in Action: New Essays in Applied Virtue Ethics* (New York: Palgrave Macmillan, 2013).
7. Aristotle, *Nicomachean Ethics*, X.9.1179b21–1180a19.
8. See L. K. Popov, D. Popov and J. Kavelin, *The Family Virtues Guide: Simple Ways to Bring Out the Best in Our Children and Ourselves* (New York: *Plume,* 1997) and Michele Borba, *Building Moral Intelligence: The Seven Essential Virtues that Teach Kids to Do the Right Thing* (Hoboken, NJ: Jossey-Bass, 2001).
9. Paula Gottlieb, "Aristotle's Ethics," in *The Oxford Handbook of the History of Ethics*, ed. Roger Crisp (Oxford: Oxford University Press, 2013), 46.
10. Hursthouse, Rosalind, "Virtue Ethics," section 1, in *Stanford Encyclopedia of Philosophy*, ed. Edward N. Zalta (Fall 2013 edn.), accessed February 27, 2016, http://plato.stanford.edu/archives/fall2013/entries/ethics-virtue/.
11. See, for example, Paul Blackledge and Kelvin Knight (eds.), *Virtue and Politics: Alasdair MacIntyre's Revolutionary Aristotelianism* (Notre Dame, IN: University of Notre Dame Press, 2011).
12. See, for example, Ronald Sandler, *Character and Environment: A Virtue-Oriented Approach to Environmental Ethics* (NY: Columbia University Press, 2007).
13. See, for example, Rosalind Hursthouse, "Virtue Theory and Abortion," *Philosophy and Public Affairs* 20, no. 3 (1991): 223–46.

GLOSSARY OF TERMS

1. **Academy:** an institution for philosophical and mathematical research founded by Plato in Athens probably in the mid-380s B.C.E.
2. *Akrasia*: a Greek word meaning "weakness of will" or "lack of mastery"; it is often translated as "incontinence." *Akrasia* is a character trait of people who seem to know the right thing to do but fail to do it.
3. **Ambulatory:** a covered area where people could walk around.
4. *Andreia*: the Greek word that, in Plato's writings, is often translated as "courage."
5. **Anthropology:** the study of human nature. "An anthropology" is a set of beliefs about what human beings are, and it often includes a notion of what allows human beings to flourish.
6. *Aretê*: a Greek word that means, literally, "excellence," most often translated in Plato and Aristotle's writings as "virtue."
7. **Biology:** the systematic study of all forms of organic life. Aristotle's biology was focused on the observation and classification of many types of marine, plant, and mammalian life.
8. **Capitalism:** a social and economic system, dominant in the West today, in which trade and industry are held in private hands and conducted for private profit.
9. **Consequentialism:** consequentialist ethics judges the morality of an action on the basis of its consequences.
10. **Contemplation:** intellectual reflection upon eternal truths. For Aristotle, contemplation is the best of activities for a human being, and the attribute that makes them unlike animals and like divine beings.
11. **Corpus:** the body of written work an author produces over his or her lifetime.
12. **Democracy:** a form of political organization in which individual citizens rule through voting for certain laws or certain representatives; the word comes from the Greek meaning "power of the people."
13. *Dikaiosune:* an ancient Greek word referring to the virtue of justice.

| Glossary of Terms

14. **Doctrine:** a philosophical doctrine is a claim that a philosopher is convinced is true; philosophical "doctrines" can be overturned by reason and argumentation.

15. *Endoxa*: a term employed by Aristotle to refer to certain opinions commonly held by the majority of the people that have passed the test of time. *Endoxa* are the starting point of moral philosophy, whose task is to make sense of them within a coherent theory.

16. **Enlightenment:** a period of rapid and widespread intellectual and cultural development in the Western world. It lasted from approximately 1650 to 1800 and brought tremendous changes in philosophy, politics, economics, and society.

17. **Epicureanism:** one of the great ancient philosophical schools founded by Epicurus (341–270 B.C.E.). Its main characteristics are materialism, and pleasure as the highest good.

18. *Ergon*: an ancient Greek word meaning "function." This concept is the basis of Aristotle's argument that the function of human beings determines the nature of the ethical life.

19. **Ethics:** the subfield of philosophy that seeks to answer the question "How should one live?" It often focuses on concepts such as right and wrong action, the virtues, and moral duty.

20. *Eudaimonia*: the end or goal toward which Aristotle argues all human life and action is aimed. It is often translated as "happiness" or "well-being" but lies somewhere between the two; like "happiness," *eudaimonia* is a state that only conscious human beings possess; like "well-being," *eudaimonia* is an objective quality of certain lives.

21. *Hedone*: Greek word for "pleasure." The word *hedonism*—seeking everything for the sake of pleasure—comes from this Greek word.

22. **Hellenistic period (322–31 B.C.E.):** a historical period in ancient Greece, during which culture and politics thrived. It ended in 31 B.C.E. when ancient Greece was displaced by the Roman Empire.

23. **Incontinence:** a common English translation of the Greek word *akrasia*, meaning "weakness of will" or "lack of mastery"—a character trait of people who seem to know the right thing to do but fail to do it.

24. **Kantian ethics:** an ethical system that follows the thought of the eighteenth-century philosopher Immanuel Kant. It is aimed at providing universal rules for action, and it proposes that an action is immoral if it cannot be willed to be done universally.

25. **Logic:** the subfield of philosophy, begun by Aristotle, which studies the nature and grounds of deductive and inductive reasoning. Aristotle's logic was focused on the strict logical relationship between terms, but logic has become much broader since Aristotle.

26. **Lyceum:** the philosophical school founded by Aristotle and in which he wrote several of his major works. It was based in Athens and continued after his death.

27. **Mean:** a mathematical term that refers to the middle between two extremes. Here the term is used non-mathematically, to mean a desirable middle ground.

28. **Medieval/Middle Ages:** the period in Western European history from about 500 C.E. to 1500 C.E. Beginning with the fall of the Roman Empire, it was a period in which both the Roman Catholic Church and Aristotle greatly influenced the realms of politics, science, and philosophy.

29. *Megalopsuchia*: literally "great-souledness"—a crowning virtue within Aristotle's system signifying the character of a person who possesses all of the other virtues, is aware of that fact, and is concerned with great expressions of honor toward himself.

30. **Metaphysics:** the subfield of philosophy focused on the nature of reality. Its literal meaning is "after physics" because Aristotle's book on the nature of reality was placed after his book on physics.

31. **Moral philosophy:** The subfield of philosophy that focuses on both the theoretical and the practical aspects of morality. It seeks primarily to answer the questions "What is the nature of the good life?" and "How ought we to live?"

32. **Neo-Aristotelians:** a group of scholars who have sought to revive Aristotle's ideas in the twentieth century. They believe in virtue ethics, an ethical theory that maintains that virtues play a central or independent role in the behavior of a person and in the moral judgment of an action.

33. **Peloponnesian War (431–404 B.C.E.):** a war fought between the city-state of Athens and its allies and the city-state of Sparta and its allies; the Spartans prevailed. The longest conflict in Greek history, it ultimately led to the weakening of the Greek cities and to their fall to foreign domination in the first century B.C.E.

34. **Peripatetics:** the followers of Aristotle; the term is a reference to *peripatos*, the Greek word for walking, possibly in reference to the ambulatory—a covered walking place—near the Lyceum.

35. **Persian Wars:** wars fought between the Persian Empire and an alliance of Greek city-states from 499 B.C.E. to 448 B.C.E. The more powerful Persians attempted to capture Athens on several occasions, but they failed to do so.

36. *Phainomena*: Greek for "appearances," or things that appear to be the case. Aristotle uses the *phainomena* and the opinions of others as the dual starting points of his philosophical investigations.

37. *Philebus*: one of Plato's late dialogues exploring the relationship of pleasure and knowledge to the good life. The speakers in the dialogue are Socrates, Protarchus, and Philebus.

38. **Philosophy:** the discipline that applies abstract and practical reasoning to the problems of human life. It addresses questions such as "How do we know the truth?", "What is the good life?", and "What is reality really like?"

39. *Phronesis*: Greek for "practical wisdom" or "prudence." Aristotle conceives of *phronesis* as an intellectual virtue that helps us to judge the right thing to do in a certain situation.

40. *Polis*: Greek for "city," usually referring to the ancient Greek city-states, such as Athens and Sparta.

41. **Pre-Socratic philosophy:** refers to the philosophers before Socrates, from

the time of Thales of Miletus (around 624–546 B.C.E.). It includes the schools of Miletus, Pythagoras, Elea, and the Atomists, and individuals such as Heraclitus and Anaxagoras, all interested in investigating the principles of the natural world.

42. **Purposive cause**: a cause aimed at bringing about some specific end. Aristotle gives these kinds of causes the name "final causes."

43. **Rationalism:** a position that emphasizes the dependence of knowledge on theoretical reason.

44. **Reason:** the human faculty of abstract reflection. Reason can be theoretical or practical, and it can deal with relations of ideas as well as with matters of fact.

45. **Renaissance:** the period of Western European history from roughly the 1500s to the beginning of the 1700s. Meaning "rebirth," the Renaissance was a period in which philosophers, artists, and authors rediscovered and put to use many of the great literary and artistic works of the Classical period of Greece and Rome.

46. **Rhetoric:** the art of persuasion by use of words. Today, it is often used negatively ("empty rhetoric"), but historically it meant good arguments and critical thinking.

47. **Roman period (27 B.C.E.–395 C.E.):** a historical period of ancient Rome, where it emerged as a great empire that dominated most of Europe.

48. **Scholasticism:** a tradition of philosophical inquiry that dominated Western philosophy in the medieval period. Scholasticism (and scholastics, the name for practitioners of Scholasticism) drew heavily on the works of Plato and Aristotle, and sought to integrate philosophy and Roman Catholic theology.

49. **Skepticism:** one of the great ancient philosophical schools, whose beginning is usually linked to the philosophy of Pyrrho of Elis (365–275 B.C.E.). Many variations appeared in history, broadly holding that nothing can be known for certain.

50. ***Sophia***: Greek for "wisdom." Aristotle uses *sophia* to name the intellectual

Glossary of Terms

faculty that helps us discover the most noble and honorable truths—something that philosophers devote themselves to.

51. **Sophist:** a professional teacher of the ancient Greek world dedicated to the mastery of excellence in several disciplines, from rhetoric to music. Plato, perhaps unfairly, portrayed the Sophists as lovers of money rather than of wisdom for wisdom's sake, and as being devoted to persuasion rather than to the discovery of truth.

52. ***Sophrosune*:** Greek for "moderation," one of the virtues in Plato's ethical works.

53. **Sparta:** an ancient Greek city-state located on the Peloponnese (a peninsula forming the southern part of modern-day Greece). Sparta and Athens were among the most powerful Greek city-states in the ancient world.

54. **Stoicism:** one of the great ancient philosophical schools, and perhaps the most influential one. Founded in Athens by Zeno of Citium in the early third century B.C.E., it has a strong moral dimension, and holds that virtue is sufficient to achieve happiness.

55. **Teleological:** related to design or purpose.

56. **Temperance:** the disposition to abstain from pleasure in the appropriate ways and in the appropriate contexts.

57. **Treatise:** a written work that deals thoroughly and systematically with a certain subject matter.

58. **Utilitarianism:** a moral philosophy developed in the nineteenth century by the English thinker Jeremy Bentham (1748–1832), which asserts that moral goodness lies exclusively in the maximizing of pleasure and the minimizing of pain for the greatest number of people.

59. **Virtue ethics:** also called "virtue-based ethics" and "agent-based ethics," this is an ethical theory that maintains the morality of an action should be judged by the character or virtue of the person, rather than by the outcome of the action (the latter being referred to as "consequentialism").

60. **Virtues:** Dispositions of character and action that both partially constitute

and make possible the good life for human beings. The virtues were important for almost every ancient moral philosopher's system, and the ancients often agreed in emphasizing practical wisdom, courage, temperance, and justice.

61. **Western world:** the civilization centered around Europe and North America that has significant cultural sources in the societies of Ancient Greece, Ancient Rome, and the Christian religion.

PEOPLE MENTIONED IN THE TEXT

1. **Alexander of Aphrodisias** was an Aristotelian philosopher and head of the Academy in Athens. He devoted his career to supporting Aristotelian philosophy against Platonism, in the form of numerous commentaries of Aristotle's works.

2. **Alexander the Great (356–323 B.C.E.)** was the son of Philip II, King of Macedon. On becoming king, Alexander started an unprecedented military campaign, conquering Persia and Egypt, reaching India, and creating one of the largest empires in the ancient world.

3. **Andronicus of Rhodes** is likely to have produced the first reliable edition of Aristotle's works. He was probably one of the leaders of the Lyceum in Athens, though there is little concrete evidence as to when.

4. **Elizabeth Anscombe (1919–2001)** was a British analytic philosopher. She worked in a variety of fields, from philosophy of mind to logic and ethics, and decisively contributed to the development of virtue ethics.

5. **Thomas Aquinas (1225–1274)** was an Italian theologian and philosopher. A member of the Dominican Order, he is arguably the most important medieval philosopher; in his extensive works he combined and blended Aristotelian philosophy and Christian theology.

6. **August Immanuel Bekker (1785–1871)** was a German philosopher and editor; he created the Bekker numbering system used for the works of Aristotle.

7. **Chris Bobonich (b. 1960)** is an American philosopher who focuses on ancient philosophy, particularly on Plato.

8. **Sarah Broadie (b. 1941)** is a professor of moral philosophy at the University of St. Andrews. Her work focuses primarily on classical philosophy, metaphysics, and ethics.

9. **Nicolaus Copernicus (1473–1543)** was a Polish astronomer and mathematician, and author of the celebrated *On the Revolutions of the Celestial Spheres*. At a pivotal moment in the intellectual history of Europe, he contributed to the scientific revolution by proposing a model of the universe with the sun at its center.

10. **René Descartes (1596–1650)** was a French philosopher and foundational thinker for modern philosophy. Descartes put forward a philosophical method of systematic doubt, and his most famous works were D*iscourse Concerning Method* (1637) and *Meditations on First Philosophy* (1641).
11. **Empedocles (circa 490–430 B.C.E.)** was a Greek philosopher who developed the famous theory of the four elements (air, fire, water, earth) by which he sought to explain natural phenomena.
12. **Epicurus (341–270 B.C.E.)**, founder of Epicureanism, was a Greek philosopher. He founded a philosophical school called "the Garden" in Athens, where, until his death, he thought and wrote down his philosophy in the form of letters.
13. **Eudoxus of Cnidus (408–355 B.C.E.)** was a Greek astronomer and mathematician. He was Plato's student and one of the greatest classical mathematicians.
14. **Philippa Foot (1920–2010)** was a British philosopher. She is best known for her work in virtue ethics.
15. **Dorothea Frede (b. 1941)** is a scholar in Classical philosophy. She is the Mills Adjunct Professor of Philosophy at the University of California at Berkeley and professor emeritus at the University of Hamburg; her primary works are on Plato, Aristotle, and Martin Heidegger.
16. **Galileo Galilei (1564–1642)** was an Italian astronomer and mathematician. One of the key figures of the scientific revolution, he was the first to observe Jupiter's satellites. He also developed modern mechanics and defended the correct belief that the earth revolves round the sun, for which he was persecuted by the Roman Catholic Church.
17. **Paula Gottlieb** is a professor of philosophy at the University of Wisconsin. Her research focuses on Aristotle's ethics and metaphysics.
18. **Heraclitus of Ephesus (circa 535–475 B.C.E.)** was a Greek philosopher. He wrote philosophy in the form of short, puzzling sentences, in which he insisted on perennial (continual) change in the natural world.
19. **Thomas Hobbes (1588–1679)** was an important philosopher in England, best known for his work in political philosophy, most notably *Leviathan* (1651).

20. **David Hume (1711–76)** was a Scottish-born philosopher and historian who played a prominent role in deemphasizing Aristotle.
21. **Rosalind Hursthouse (b. 1943)** is a philosopher from New Zealand. She has followed the path of her mentors, Anscombe and Foot, in developing virtue ethics.
22. **Terence Irwin (b. 1947)** is a professor of ancient philosophy at Oxford University. His work focuses primarily on how ethics developed in the ancient world.
23. **Immanuel Kant (1724–1804)** was a German Enlightenment philosopher. He wrote the celebrated *Critique of Pure Reason* and *Critique of Practical Reason*, originated the Kantian school, and decisively influenced German Idealism and ethics.
24. **Alasdair MacIntyre (b. 1929)** is a Scottish philosopher and senior research fellow at London Metropolitan University. His 1981 text *After Virtue* is considered groundbreaking.
25. **J. L. Mackie (1917–81)** was an Australian philosopher who specialized in moral and political philosophy. His most important works include *The Miracle of Theism* (1982) and *Ethics: Inventing Right and Wrong* (1977).
26. **Albertus Magnus (1200–1280)** is the Latin name for "Albert the Great"—one of the most important Roman Catholic philosophers and theologians in the Middle Ages. He helped integrate Aristotle's teaching into Catholic Christianity, and his most important works include two commentaries on Aristotle's *Nicomachean Ethics*.
27. **Martha Nussbaum (b. 1947)** is an American philosopher. She has worked in ancient philosophy, political philosophy, feminism, and animal rights; she is highly influential both within and outside of the academic world.
28. **Parmenides of Elea (b. circa 540 B.C.E.)** was a Greek philosopher. He is one of the most influential pre-Socratic philosophers, and he argued for the metaphysical unity of all reality, whose distinctions and differences are only appearances.

29. **Plato (427–347 B.C.E.)** was a Greek philosopher. Founder of the Academy in Athens, and one of the greatest philosophers of the Western tradition, he was a disciple of Socrates and teacher of Aristotle. He wrote the great *Dialogues* (including *Republic* and *Symposium*) that set the agenda for Western philosophy.
30. **Ronald Polansky (b. 1949)** is a professor of philosophy at Duquesne University and the editor of the journal *Ancient Philosophy*.
31. **Anthony Preus** is a professor of philosophy at Binghamton University, where he teaches courses on ancient philosophy and the works of Aristotle, Plato, and Socrates.
32. **Socrates (469–399 B.C.E.)** was an Athenian philosopher and the teacher of Plato. He was sentenced to death in 399 B.C.E. on charges of introducing new gods and corrupting the youth. While he did not leave any written texts, Plato's account of his philosophical method of searching for the proper definition of things is acknowledged as a pivotal moment in Western philosophy.
33. **Speusippus (circa. 408–339 B.C.E.)** was a Greek philosopher. He was Plato's nephew and Plato's first successor as head of the Academy.
34. **Francisco Suarez (1548–1617)** was a very influential Spanish theologian and philosopher, whose most famous works include *Metaphysical Disputations* (1597) and *On the Laws* (1612).
35. **Theophrastus (circa 371–circa 287 B.C.E.)** was a Greek philosopher, disciple of Aristotle, and successor to Aristotle at his philosophical school, the Lyceum.
36. **Bernard Williams (1929–2003)** was a highly influential British moral philosopher in the second half of the twentieth century. His most important works include *Ethics and the Limits of Philosophy* (1985) and *Utilitarianism: For and Against* (1973).

WORKS CITED

1. Anagnostopoulos, Georgios. "Aristotle's Works and the Development of His Thought." In *A Companion to Aristotle*, edited by Georgios Anagnostopoulos. Oxford: Wiley-Blackwell, 2009.
2. Anscombe, G. E. M. "Modern Moral Philosophy." *Philosophy* 33, no. 124 (1958): 1–19.
3. Aristotle. *The Complete Works of Aristotle*. Edited by Jonathan Barnes. Princeton, NJ: Princeton University Press, 1991.
4. ———. *Eudemian Ethics*. Edited by Brad Inwood and Raphael Woolf. Cambridge: Cambridge University Press, 2013.
5. ———. *Metaphysics*. New York: Peripatetic Press, 1979.
6. ———. *Metaphysics*. Translated by S. M. Cohen. In *Readings in Ancient Greek Philosophy*, edited by S. Cohen, P. Curd and C. D. C. Reeve. Indianapolis: Hackett, 2005.
7. ———. *Nicomachean Ethics*, rev. ed. Translated by Roger Crisp. Cambridge: Cambridge University Press, 2014.
8. ———. *Physics*. Lincoln: University of Nebraska, 1961.
9. ———. *Politics*. Translated by T. Irwin. In *Readings in Ancient Greek Philosophy*, edited by S. Cohen, P. Curd and C. D. C. Reeve. Indianapolis: Hackett, 2005.
10. Austin, Michael. *Virtues in Action: New Essays in Applied Virtue Ethics*. New York: Palgrave Macmillan, 2013.
11. Barnes, Jonathan. *Aristotle Complete Works*. Princeton, NJ: Princeton University Press, 1991.
12. ———. *The Cambridge Companion to Aristotle*. Cambridge: Cambridge University Press, 1995.
13. Blackledge, Paul, and Kelvin Knight (eds.). *Virtue and Politics: Alasdair MacIntyre's Revolutionary Aristotelianism*. Notre Dame, IN: University of Notre Dame Press, 2011.
14. Bobonich, Chris. "Aristotle's Ethical Treatises." In *The Blackwell Guide to Aristotle's Nicomachean Ethics*, edited by Richard Kraut, 12–36. Oxford: Wiley-Blackwell, 2006.
15. Borba, Michele. *Building Moral Intelligence: The Seven Essential Virtues that*

Teach Kids to Do the Right Thing. Hoboken, NJ: Jossey-Bass, 2001.

16. Broadie, Sarah. "Aristotle and Contemporary Ethics." In *The Blackwell Guide to Aristotle's Nicomachean Ethics*, edited by Richard Kraut, 342–61. Oxford: Wiley-Blackwell, 2006.

17. ———. "Philosophical Introduction." In Aristotle, *Nicomachean Ethics*, translated by Sarah Broadie and Christopher Rowe, 9–80. Oxford: Oxford University Press, 2002.

18. Celano, Anthony. "The Relation of Prudence and *Synderesis* to Happiness in the Medieval Commentaries on Aristotle's Ethics." In *The Reception of Aristotle's Ethics*, edited by Jon Miller, 125–54. Cambridge: Cambridge University Press, 2012.

19. Cooper, J. M. "Contemplation and Happiness: A Reconsideration." In *Reason and Emotion: Essays on Ancient Moral Psychology and Ethical Theory*. Princeton, NJ: Princeton University Press, 1999.

20. ———. "The *Magna Moralia* and Aristotle's Moral Philosophy." *American Journal of Philology* (1973): 327–49.

21. Copleston, Frederick. *A History of Philosophy: Greece and Rome*. London: Continuum Press, 2003.

22. Crisp, Roger. *Aristotle Nicomachean Ethics*. Cambridge: *Cambridge University Press*, 2014.

23. Crisp, Roger, and M. A. Slote (eds.). *Virtue Ethics.* Oxford: Oxford University Press, 1997.

24. Diogenes Laertius. *Lives of Eminent Philosophers*. Edited by R. D. Hicks. Cambridge, MA: Harvard University Press, 1966.

25. Finnis, John. "Aquinas's Moral, Political, and Legal Philosophy." In *Stanford Encyclopedia of Philosophy* (Summer 2014 edn.), edited by Edward N. Zalta. Accessed 15 January, 2016. http://plato.stanford.edu/archives/sum2014/ entries/aquinas-moral-political/.

26. Frede, Dorothea. "Pleasure and Pain in Aristotle's Ethics." In *The Blackwell Guide to Aristotle's Nicomachean Ethics*, edited by R. Kraut, 255–75. Oxford: Blackwell Publishing, 2006.

27. Gauthier, R. A. "Trois commentaries 'averroistes' sur l'Ethique a Nicomaque." *Archives d'histoire doctrinale et litteraire du moyen age* 16, no. 1 (1947–8):

187–336.
28. Gottlieb, Paula. "Aristotle's Ethics." In *The Oxford Handbook of the History of Ethics*, edited by R. Crisp. Oxford: Oxford University Press, 2013.
29. Herdt, Jennifer A. "Aquinas's Aristotelian Defense of Martyr Courage." In *Aquinas and the* Nicomachean Ethics, edited by Tobias Hoffman, Jorn Muller and Matthias Perkams. Cambridge: Cambridge University Press, 2013.
30. Hoffmann, Tobias, Jörn Müller and Matthias Perkams (eds.). *Aquinas and the* Nicomachean Ethics. Cambridge: Cambridge University Press, 2013.
31. Holowchack, M. Andrew. *Happiness and Greek Ethical Thought*. London: Continuum Press, 2005.
32. Hursthouse, Rosalind. *On Virtue Ethics*. Oxford: Oxford University Press, 2001.
33. ———. "Virtue Ethics." In *Stanford Encyclopedia of Philosophy* (Fall 2013 edn.), edited by Edward N. Zalta,. Accessed February 27, 2016. http://plato.stanford.edu/ archives/fall2013/entries/ethics-virtue/.
34. ———. "Virtue Theory and Abortion." *Philosophy and Public Affairs* 20, no. 3 (1991): 223–46.
35. Irwin, Terence. *The Development of Ethics*, vol. 1. Oxford: Oxford University Press, 2007.
36. Kenny, Anthony. *The Aristotelian Ethics: A Study of the Relationship Between the* Eudemian *and* Nicomachean Ethics *of Aristotle*. Oxford: Clarendon Press, 1978.
37. Korsgaard, Christine. *Sources of Normativity*. Cambridge: Cambridge University Press, 2012.
38. Kraut, R. (ed.) *The Blackwell Guide to Aristotle's* Nicomachean Ethics. Oxford: Blackwell, 2006.
39. ———. "Two Conceptions of Happiness." *The Philosophical Review* 88 (1979): 167–97.
40. Long, A. A. "Aristotle's Legacy to Stoic Ethics." *Bulletin of the Institute of Classical Study* 15, no. 1 (1968): 72–85.
41. MacIntyre, Alasdair. *After Virtue*, 3rd edn. Notre Dame: University of Notre Dame Press, 2007.
42. ———. *Whose Justice? Which Rationality?* London: Duckworth, 1988.

43. Mackie, J. L. *Ethics: Inventing Right and Wrong*. London: Penguin, 1977.
44. McAleer, Sean. "An Aristotelian Account of Virtue Ethics." *Pacific Philosophical Quarterly* 88 (2007): 208–25.
45. McInerny, Ralph, and John O'Callaghan. "Saint Thomas Aquinas." In *Stanford Encyclopedia of Philosophy* (May 23, 2014). Edited by Edward N. Zalta. Accessed December 10, 2015. http://plato.stanford.edu/entries/ aquinas/#ThoAri.
46. Mourelatos, Alexander (ed.) *The Pre-Socratics: A Collection of Critical Essays*. Princeton, NJ: Princeton University Press, 1993.
47. Nielsen, Karen M. "The *Nicomachean Ethics* in Hellenistic Philosophy—A Hidden Treasure?" In *The Reception of Aristotle's Ethics*, edited by Jon Miller, 5–30. Cambridge: Cambridge University Press, 2012.
48. Nussbaum, M. C. "Non-Relative Virtues: An Aristotelian Approach." In *The Quality of Life*, edited by M. C. Nussbaum and A. Sen, 242–69. Oxford: Clarendon Press, 1993.
49. ———. "Non-Relative Virtues: An Aristotelian Approach." *Midwest Studies in Philosophy* 13, no. 1 (1998): 34.
50. ———. "Virtue Ethics: A Misleading Category?" *Journal of Ethics* 3, no. 3 (1999): 163–201.
51. Plato. *The Republic*. Translated by G. M. A. Grube. In *Readings in Ancient Greek Philosophy*, edited by S. Cohen, P. Curd and C. D. C. Reeve. Indianapolis: Hackett, 2005.
52. Polansky, Ronald (ed.) *The Cambridge Companion to Aristotle's* Nicomachean Ethics. Cambridge: Cambridge University Press, 2014.
53. ———. "Introduction: Ethics as Practical Science." In *The Cambridge Companion to Aristotle's Nicomachean Ethics*, edited by R. Polansky. Cambridge: Cambridge University Press, 2014.
54. Popov, L. K., D. Popov and J. Kavelin. *The Family Virtues Guide: Simple Ways to Bring out the Best in Our Children and Ourselves*. New York: Plume, 1997.
55. Preus, Anthony. *Historical Dictionary of Ancient Greek Philosophy*. Lanham, MD: Scarecrow Press, 2007.
56. Ross, David. *The Nicomachean Ethics of Aristotle*. Claremont, CA: Pomona Press, 2006.
57. Rowe, C. "A Reply to John Cooper on the Magna Moralia." *American Journal of*

Philology (1975): 160–72.

58. Rutherford, Donald. "The End of Ends? Aristotelian Themes in Early Modern Ethics." In *The Reception of Aristotle's Ethics*, edited by Jon Miller, 194–221. Cambridge: Cambridge University Press, 2013.

59. Sandler, Ronald. *Character and Environment: A Virtue-Oriented Approach to Environmental Ethics*. New York: Columbia University Press, 2007.

60. Shields, Christopher. "Aristotle." In *Stanford Encyclopedia of Philosophy* (Fall 2015 edn.). Edited by Edward N. Zalta. Accessed January 15, 2015, http:// plato.stanford.edu/archives/fall2015/entries/aristotle/.

61. Williams, Bernard. *Ethics and the Limits of Philosophy*. London: Routledge, 2006.

原书作者简介

亚里士多德,公元前 384 年出生于马其顿,17 岁时移居希腊雅典,开始跟随柏拉图学习哲学。柏拉图是欧洲哲学的奠基者之一,亚里士多德求学的地方就是著名的柏拉图学园(又译"阿卡德米")。柏拉图于公元前 347 年逝世后,亚里士多德返回马其顿,教导年轻的亚历山大大帝。公元前 335 年,他重返雅典创立自己的学校,校名为吕克昂。公元前 322 年,因政治动乱,亚里士多德不得不再次离开雅典,不久后逝世于埃维厄岛。

本书作者简介

乔瓦尼·盖勒博士于格拉斯哥大学获博士学位,研究内容为 17 世纪苏格兰对亚里士多德思想的认识。盖勒博士现为该校博士后研究员,研究方向为早期现代哲学和科学。

乔恩·汤普森任教于伦敦国王学院哲学系,现于该校攻读博士学位。

世界名著中的批判性思维

《世界思想宝库钥匙丛书》致力于深入浅出地阐释全世界著名思想家的观点,不论是谁、在何处都能了解到,从而推进批判性思维发展。

《世界思想宝库钥匙丛书》与世界顶尖大学的一流学者合作,为一系列学科中最有影响的著作推出新的分析文本,介绍其观点和影响。在这一不断扩展的系列中,每种选入的著作都代表了历经时间考验的思想典范。通过为这些著作提供必要背景、揭示原作者的学术渊源以及说明这些著作所产生的影响,本系列图书希望让读者以新视角看待这些划时代的经典之作。读者应学会思考、运用并挑战这些著作中的观点,而不是简单接受它们。

ABOUT THE AUTHOR OF THE ORIGINAL WORK

Aristotle was born in 384 B.C.E., in what is present-day Macedonia. At the age of 17 he moved to Athens in Greece to begin an education in philosophy under Plato, one of the founders of European philosophy, at his renowned Academy. On Plato's death in 347 B.C.E., Aristotle moved back to Macedonia to tutor the young Alexander the Great. But in 335 B.C.E. he returned to Athens and established his own school, the Lyceum. Political unrest forced Aristotle to leave Athens again in 322 B.C.E., and he died shortly afterwards on the island of Euboea.

ABOUT THE AUTHORS OF THE ANALYSIS

Dr Giovanni Gellera holds a doctorate from the University of Glasgow on the reception of Aristotle in seventeenth-century Scotland. He is curently a postdoctoral researcher in early modern philosophy and science at his alma mater.
Jon W. Thompson teaches in the Department of Philosophy at King's College London, where he is currently a PhD candidate.

ABOUT MACAT
GREAT WORKS FOR CRITICAL THINKING

Macat is focused on making the ideas of the world's great thinkers accessible and comprehensible to everybody, everywhere, in ways that promote the development of enhanced critical thinking skills.

It works with leading academics from the world's top universities to produce new analyses that focus on the ideas and the impact of the most influential works ever written across a wide variety of academic disciplines. Each of the works that sit at the heart of its growing library is an enduring example of great thinking. But by setting them in context—and looking at the influences that shaped their authors, as well as the responses they provoked—Macat encourages readers to look at these classics and game-changers with fresh eyes. Readers learn to think, engage and challenge their ideas, rather than simply accepting them.

批判性思维和《尼各马可伦理学》

主要批判性思维技能：理性化思维

次要批判性思维技能：评估

在《尼各马可伦理学》中，亚里士多德展示了一位思想家的思维能力，他的文字逻辑清晰、条理清楚、论证严密。

亚里士多德非常注重辨析伦理行为的特征，他致力于探索道德生活的构成要素。如果只就他叙述宏大、论证严密的观点而言，一般人都会觉得这位古希腊思想家是一位"难懂"的哲学家。但是，我们认为难懂的地方——他严谨、固执的论证过程——也可以看做是他思维清晰的优点。他使用假设论证的方法，达到了很好的效果：如果一个人拥有一种美德，那他就拥有所有的美德。因为如果一个人有某种得到充分发展的美德，他就会拥有"实践智慧"；而如果他拥有实践智慧，他就拥有所有的美德。

亚里士多德的论证过程也有驳论。在为善的（成功的）生活辩护时，他详细地驳斥了柏拉图的善的理念，认为它是难以实现的。总体来说，柏拉图和亚里士多德对于美德的看法是不一致的。亚里士多德的美德，更强调获取政治、经济上的成功以及智慧。在严谨的论证中，亚里士多德也密切地关注到他所使用的一些术语的含义，如"实践智慧"、"政治智慧"等。《尼各马可伦理学》是一部独一无二的著作，它是丰富的批判性思维技巧的产物，深入地探讨了美德、理性和人的至善等问题。更重要的是，这些探讨的内容，奠定了流传至今的西方文明核心价值的基础。

CRITICAL THINKING AND *NICOMACHEAN ETHICS*

- Primary critical thinking skill: REASONING
- Secondary critical thinking skill: EVALUATION

In *Nicomachean Ethics*, Aristotle shows himself to be a fine example of a thinker whose writing is clearly and coherently reasoned.

Very much concerned with identifying the features of ethical behaviour, Aristotle wanted to know what makes an ethical life. Providing, as he does, epic, rigorously-reasoned arguments, the Greek thinker is generally recognised as a "difficult" philosopher. But what can be taken for difficulty—the density and persistence of his argumentation—can also be seen as a strong feature of its clarity. He uses hypothetical argumentation to good effect: if a man has one of the virtues, then he must have all of them since, if he has a fully developed virtue, then he has "practical wisdom;" if he has such wisdom, then he has all the virtues.

Aristotle also deals with counter-arguments in his reasoning. In his argument for the good (or successful) life, he carefully argues against Plato's Idea of the Good on the basis that it's not achievable and, anyway, it is not something that fits with Aristotle's stress on the virtue of achieving success in politics, economics and wisdom. His careful argumentation also pays close attention to the meaning of the terms that he uses, such as "practical wisdom" and "political wisdom". The unique product of a rich deployment of key critical thinking skills, *Nicomachean Ethics* comprises a rich exploration of virtue, reason and the ultimate human good-an exploration, moreover, that forms the basis of the values that lie at the heart of Western civilization to this day.

《世界思想宝库钥匙丛书》简介

　　《世界思想宝库钥匙丛书》致力于为一系列在各领域产生重大影响的人文社科类经典著作提供独特的学术探讨。每一本读物都不仅仅是原经典著作的内容摘要，而是介绍并深入研究原经典著作的学术渊源、主要观点和历史影响。这一丛书的目的是提供一套学习资料，以促进读者掌握批判性思维，从而更全面、深刻地去理解重要思想。

　　每一本读物分为3个部分：学术渊源、学术思想和学术影响，每个部分下有4个小节。这些章节旨在从各个方面研究原经典著作及其反响。

　　由于独特的体例，每一本读物不但易于阅读，而且另有一项优点：所有读物的编排体例相同，读者在进行某个知识层面的调查或研究时可交叉参阅多本该丛书中的相关读物，从而开启跨领域研究的路径。

　　为了方便阅读，每本读物最后还列出了术语表和人名表（在书中则以星号＊标记），此外还有参考文献。

　　《世界思想宝库钥匙丛书》与剑桥大学合作，理清了批判性思维的要点，即如何通过6种技能来进行有效思考。其中3种技能让我们能够理解问题，另3种技能让我们有能力解决问题。这6种技能合称为"批判性思维PACIER模式"，它们是：

分析：了解如何建立一个观点；
评估：研究一个观点的优点和缺点；
阐释：对意义所产生的问题加以理解；
创造性思维：提出新的见解，发现新的联系；
解决问题：提出切实有效的解决办法；
理性化思维：创建有说服力的观点。

了解更多信息，请浏览 www.macat.com。

THE MACAT LIBRARY

The Macat Library is a series of unique academic explorations of seminal works in the humanities and social sciences — books and papers that have had a significant and widely recognised impact on their disciplines. It has been created to serve as much more than just a summary of what lies between the covers of a great book. It illuminates and explores the influences on, ideas of, and impact of that book. Our goal is to offer a learning resource that encourages critical thinking and fosters a better, deeper understanding of important ideas.

Each publication is divided into three Sections: Influences, Ideas, and Impact. Each Section has four Modules. These explore every important facet of the work, and the responses to it.

This Section-Module structure makes a Macat Library book easy to use, but it has another important feature. Because each Macat book is written to the same format, it is possible (and encouraged!) to cross-reference multiple Macat books along the same lines of inquiry or research. This allows the reader to open up interesting interdisciplinary pathways.

To further aid your reading, lists of glossary terms and people mentioned are included at the end of this book (these are indicated by an asterisk [*] throughout) — as well as a list of works cited.

Macat has worked with the University of Cambridge to identify the elements of critical thinking and understand the ways in which six different skills combine to enable effective thinking.

Three allow us to fully understand a problem; three more give us the tools to solve it. Together, these six skills make up the PACIER model of critical thinking. They are:

ANALYSIS — understanding how an argument is built
EVALUATION — exploring the strengths and weaknesses of an argument
INTERPRETATION — understanding issues of meaning
CREATIVE THINKING — coming up with new ideas and fresh connections
PROBLEM-SOLVING — producing strong solutions
REASONING — creating strong arguments

To find out more, visit WWW.MACAT.COM.

"《世界思想宝库钥匙丛书》提供了独一无二的跨学科学习和研究工具。它介绍那些革新了各自学科研究的经典著作,还邀请全世界一流专家和教育机构进行严谨的分析,为每位读者打开世界顶级教育的大门。"

—— 安德烈亚斯·施莱歇尔,
经济合作与发展组织教育与技能司司长

"《世界思想宝库钥匙丛书》直面大学教育的巨大挑战……他们组建了一支精干而活跃的学者队伍,来推出在研究广度上颇具新意的教学材料。"

—— 布罗尔斯教授、勋爵,剑桥大学前校长

"《世界思想宝库钥匙丛书》的愿景令人赞叹。它通过分析和阐释那些曾深刻影响人类思想以及社会、经济发展的经典文本,提供了新的学习方法。它推动批判性思维,这对于任何社会和经济体来说都是至关重要的。这就是未来的学习方法。"

—— 查尔斯·克拉克阁下,英国前教育大臣

"对于那些影响了各自领域的著作,《世界思想宝库钥匙丛书》能让人们立即了解到围绕那些著作展开的评论性言论,这让该系列图书成为在这些领域从事研究的师生们不可或缺的资源。"

—— 威廉·特朗佐教授,加利福尼亚大学圣地亚哥分校

"Macat offers an amazing first-of-its-kind tool for interdisciplinary learning and research. Its focus on works that transformed their disciplines and its rigorous approach, drawing on the world's leading experts and educational institutions, opens up a world-class education to anyone."

—— Andreas Schleicher, Director for Education and Skills, Organisation for Economic Co-operation and Development

"Macat is taking on some of the major challenges in university education... They have drawn together a strong team of active academics who are producing teaching materials that are novel in the breadth of their approach."

—— Prof Lord Broers, former Vice-Chancellor of the University of Cambridge

"The Macat vision is exceptionally exciting. It focuses upon new modes of learning which analyse and explain seminal texts which have profoundly influenced world thinking and so social and economic development. It promotes the kind of critical thinking which is essential for any society and economy. This is the learning of the future."

—— Rt Hon Charles Clarke, former UK Secretary of State for Education

"The Macat analyses provide immediate access to the critical conversation surrounding the books that have shaped their respective discipline, which will make them an invaluable resource to all of those, students and teachers, working in the field."

—— Prof William Tronzo, University of California at San Diego

The Macat Library
世界思想宝库钥匙丛书

TITLE	中文书名	类别
An Analysis of Arjun Appadurai's *Modernity at Large: Cultural Dimensions of Globalization*	解析阿尔君·阿帕杜莱《消失的现代性：全球化的文化维度》	人类学
An Analysis of Claude Lévi-Strauss's *Structural Anthropology*	解析克劳德·列维-斯特劳斯《结构人类学》	人类学
An Analysis of Marcel Mauss's *The Gift*	解析马塞尔·莫斯《礼物》	人类学
An Analysis of Jared M. Diamond's *Guns, Germs, and Steel: The Fate of Human Societies*	解析贾雷德·M.戴蒙德《枪炮、病菌与钢铁：人类社会的命运》	人类学
An Analysis of Clifford Geertz's *The Interpretation of Cultures*	解析克利福德·格尔茨《文化的解释》	人类学
An Analysis of Philippe Ariès's *Centuries of Childhood: A Social History of Family Life*	解析菲力浦·阿利埃斯《儿童的世纪：旧制度下的儿童和家庭生活》	人类学
An Analysis of W. Chan Kim & Renée Mauborgne's *Blue Ocean Strategy*	解析金伟灿/勒妮·莫博涅《蓝海战略》	商业
An Analysis of John P. Kotter's *Leading Change*	解析约翰·P.科特《领导变革》	商业
An Analysis of Michael E. Porter's *Competitive Strategy: Techniques for Analyzing Industries and Competitors*	解析迈克尔·E.波特《竞争战略：分析产业和竞争对手的技术》	商业
An Analysis of Jean Lave & Etienne Wenger's *Situated Learning: Legitimate Peripheral Participation*	解析琼·莱夫/艾蒂纳·温格《情境学习：合法的边缘性参与》	商业
An Analysis of Douglas McGregor's *The Human Side of Enterprise*	解析道格拉斯·麦格雷戈《企业的人性面》	商业
An Analysis of Milton Friedman's *Capitalism and Freedom*	解析米尔顿·弗里德曼《资本主义与自由》	商业
An Analysis of Ludwig von Mises's *The Theory of Money and Credit*	解析路德维希·冯·米塞斯《货币和信用理论》	经济学
An Analysis of Adam Smith's *The Wealth of Nations*	解析亚当·斯密《国富论》	经济学
An Analysis of Thomas Piketty's *Capital in the Twenty-First Century*	解析托马斯·皮凯蒂《21世纪资本论》	经济学
An Analysis of Nassim Nicholas Taleb's *The Black Swan: The Impact of the Highly Improbable*	解析纳西姆·尼古拉斯·塔勒布《黑天鹅：如何应对不可预知的未来》	经济学
An Analysis of Ha-Joon Chang's *Kicking Away the Ladder*	解析张夏准《富国陷阱：发达国家为何踢开梯子》	经济学
An Analysis of Thomas Robert Malthus's *An Essay on the Principle of Population*	解析托马斯·罗伯特·马尔萨斯《人口论》	经济学

An Analysis of John Maynard Keynes's *The General Theory of Employment, Interest and Money*	解析约翰·梅纳德·凯恩斯《就业、利息和货币通论》	经济学
An Analysis of Milton Friedman's *The Role of Monetary Policy*	解析米尔顿·弗里德曼《货币政策的作用》	经济学
An Analysis of Burton G. Malkiel's *A Random Walk Down Wall Street*	解析伯顿·G. 马尔基尔《漫步华尔街》	经济学
An Analysis of Friedrich A. Hayek's *The Road to Serfdom*	解析弗里德里希·A. 哈耶克《通往奴役之路》	经济学
An Analysis of Charles P. Kindleberger's *Manias, Panics, and Crashes: A History of Financial Crises*	解析查尔斯·P. 金德尔伯格《疯狂、惊恐和崩溃：金融危机史》	经济学
An Analysis of Amartya Sen's *Development as Freedom*	解析阿马蒂亚·森《以自由看待发展》	经济学
An Analysis of Rachel Carson's *Silent Spring*	解析蕾切尔·卡森《寂静的春天》	地理学
An Analysis of Charles Darwin's *On the Origin of Species: by Means of Natural Selection, or The Preservation of Favoured Races in the Struggle for Life*	解析查尔斯·达尔文《物种起源》	地理学
An Analysis of World Commission on Environment and Development's *The Brundtland Report: Our Common Future*	解析世界环境与发展委员会《布伦特兰报告：我们共同的未来》	地理学
An Analysis of James E. Lovelock's *Gaia: A New Look at Life on Earth*	解析詹姆斯·E. 拉伍洛克《盖娅：地球生命的新视野》	地理学
An Analysis of Paul Kennedy's *The Rise and Fall of the Great Powers: Economic Change and Military Conflict from 1500–2000*	解析保罗·肯尼迪《大国的兴衰：1500—2000年的经济变革与军事冲突》	历史
An Analysis of Janet L. Abu-Lughod's *Before European Hegemony: The World System A. D. 1250–1350*	解析珍妮特·L. 阿布-卢格霍德《欧洲霸权之前：1250—1350年的世界体系》	历史
An Analysis of Alfred W. Crosby's *The Columbian Exchange: Biological and Cultural Consequences of 1492*	解析艾尔弗雷德·W. 克罗斯比《哥伦布大交换：1492年以后的生物影响和文化冲击》	历史
An Analysis of Tony Judt's *Postwar: A History of Europe since 1945*	解析托尼·朱特《战后欧洲史》	历史
An Analysis of Richard J. Evans's *In Defence of History*	解析理查德·J. 艾文斯《捍卫历史》	历史
An Analysis of Eric Hobsbawm's *The Age of Revolution: Europe 1789–1848*	解析艾瑞克·霍布斯鲍姆《革命的年代：欧洲1789—1848年》	历史

An Analysis of Roland Barthes's *Mythologies*	解析罗兰·巴特《神话学》	文学与批判理论
An Analysis of Simone de Beauvoir's *The Second Sex*	解析西蒙娜·德·波伏娃《第二性》	文学与批判理论
An Analysis of Edward W. Said's *Orientalism*	解析爱德华·W. 萨义德《东方主义》	文学与批判理论
An Analysis of Virginia Woolf's *A Room of One's Own*	解析弗吉尼亚·伍尔芙《一间自己的房间》	文学与批判理论
An Analysis of Judith Butler's *Gender Trouble*	解析朱迪斯·巴特勒《性别麻烦》	文学与批判理论
An Analysis of Ferdinand de Saussure's *Course in General Linguistics*	解析费尔迪南·德·索绪尔《普通语言学教程》	文学与批判理论
An Analysis of Susan Sontag's *On Photography*	解析苏珊·桑塔格《论摄影》	文学与批判理论
An Analysis of Walter Benjamin's *The Work of Art in the Age of Mechanical Reproduction*	解析瓦尔特·本雅明《机械复制时代的艺术作品》	文学与批判理论
An Analysis of W. E. B. Du Bois's *The Souls of Black Folk*	解析 W.E.B. 杜波依斯《黑人的灵魂》	文学与批判理论
An Analysis of Plato's *The Republic*	解析柏拉图《理想国》	哲学
An Analysis of Plato's *Symposium*	解析柏拉图《会饮篇》	哲学
An Analysis of Aristotle's *Metaphysics*	解析亚里士多德《形而上学》	哲学
An Analysis of Aristotle's *Nicomachean Ethics*	解析亚里士多德《尼各马可伦理学》	哲学
An Analysis of Immanuel Kant's *Critique of Pure Reason*	解析伊曼努尔·康德《纯粹理性批判》	哲学
An Analysis of Ludwig Wittgenstein's *Philosophical Investigations*	解析路德维希·维特根斯坦《哲学研究》	哲学
An Analysis of G. W. F. Hegel's *Phenomenology of Spirit*	解析 G.W.F. 黑格尔《精神现象学》	哲学
An Analysis of Baruch Spinoza's *Ethics*	解析巴鲁赫·斯宾诺莎《伦理学》	哲学
An Analysis of Hannah Arendt's *The Human Condition*	解析汉娜·阿伦特《人的境况》	哲学
An Analysis of G. E. M. Anscombe's *Modern Moral Philosophy*	解析 G.E.M. 安斯康姆《现代道德哲学》	哲学
An Analysis of David Hume's *An Enquiry Concerning Human Understanding*	解析大卫·休谟《人类理解研究》	哲学

An Analysis of Søren Kierkegaard's *Fear and Trembling*	解析索伦·克尔凯郭尔《恐惧与战栗》	哲学
An Analysis of René Descartes's *Meditations on First Philosophy*	解析勒内·笛卡尔《第一哲学沉思录》	哲学
An Analysis of Friedrich Nietzsche's *On the Genealogy of Morality*	解析弗里德里希·尼采《论道德的谱系》	哲学
An Analysis of Gilbert Ryle's *The Concept of Mind*	解析吉尔伯特·赖尔《心的概念》	哲学
An Analysis of Thomas Kuhn's *The Structure of Scientific Revolutions*	解析托马斯·库恩《科学革命的结构》	哲学
An Analysis of John Stuart Mill's *Utilitarianism*	解析约翰·斯图亚特·穆勒《功利主义》	哲学
An Analysis of Aristotle's *Politics*	解析亚里士多德《政治学》	政治学
An Analysis of Niccolò Machiavelli's *The Prince*	解析尼科洛·马基雅维利《君主论》	政治学
An Analysis of Karl Marx's *Capital*	解析卡尔·马克思《资本论》	政治学
An Analysis of Benedict Anderson's *Imagined Communities*	解析本尼迪克特·安德森《想象的共同体》	政治学
An Analysis of Samuel P. Huntington's *The Clash of Civilizations and the Remaking of World Order*	解析塞缪尔·P.亨廷顿《文明的冲突与世界秩序的重建》	政治学
An Analysis of Alexis de Tocqueville's *Democracy in America*	解析阿列克西·德·托克维尔《论美国的民主》	政治学
An Analysis of John A. Hobson's *Imperialism: A Study*	解析约翰·A.霍布森《帝国主义》	政治学
An Analysis of Thomas Paine's *Common Sense*	解析托马斯·潘恩《常识》	政治学
An Analysis of John Rawls's *A Theory of Justice*	解析约翰·罗尔斯《正义论》	政治学
An Analysis of Francis Fukuyama's *The End of History and the Last Man*	解析弗朗西斯·福山《历史的终结与最后的人》	政治学
An Analysis of John Locke's *Two Treatises of Government*	解析约翰·洛克《政府论》	政治学
An Analysis of Sun Tzu's *The Art of War*	解析孙武《孙子兵法》	政治学
An Analysis of Henry Kissinger's *World Order: Reflections on the Character of Nations and the Course of History*	解析亨利·基辛格《世界秩序》	政治学
An Analysis of Jean-Jacques Rousseau's *The Social Contract*	解析让-雅克·卢梭《社会契约论》	政治学

An Analysis of Odd Arne Westad's *The Global Cold War: Third World Interventions and the Making of Our Times*	解析文安立《全球冷战：美苏对第三世界的干涉与当代世界的形成》	政治学
An Analysis of Sigmund Freud's *The Interpretation of Dreams*	解析西格蒙德·弗洛伊德《梦的解析》	心理学
An Analysis of William James' *The Principles of Psychology*	解析威廉·詹姆斯《心理学原理》	心理学
An Analysis of Philip Zimbardo's *The Lucifer Effect*	解析菲利普·津巴多《路西法效应》	心理学
An Analysis of Leon Festinger's *A Theory of Cognitive Dissonance*	解析利昂·费斯汀格《认知失调论》	心理学
An Analysis of Richard H. Thaler & Cass R. Sunstein's *Nudge: Improving Decisions about Health, Wealth, and Happiness*	解析理查德·H. 泰勒/卡斯·R. 桑斯坦《助推：如何做出有关健康、财富和幸福的更优决策》	心理学
An Analysis of Gordon Allport's *The Nature of Prejudice*	解析高尔登·奥尔波特《偏见的本质》	心理学
An Analysis of Steven Pinker's *The Better Angels of Our Nature: Why Violence Has Declined*	解析斯蒂芬·平克《人性中的善良天使：暴力为什么会减少》	心理学
An Analysis of Stanley Milgram's *Obedience to Authority*	解析斯坦利·米尔格拉姆《对权威的服从》	心理学
An Analysis of Betty Friedan's *The Feminine Mystique*	解析贝蒂·弗里丹《女性的奥秘》	心理学
An Analysis of David Riesman's *The Lonely Crowd: A Study of the Changing American Character*	解析大卫·理斯曼《孤独的人群：美国人社会性格演变之研究》	社会学
An Analysis of Franz Boas's *Race, Language and Culture*	解析弗朗兹·博厄斯《种族、语言与文化》	社会学
An Analysis of Pierre Bourdieu's *Outline of a Theory of Practice*	解析皮埃尔·布尔迪厄《实践理论大纲》	社会学
An Analysis of Max Weber's *The Protestant Ethic and the Spirit of Capitalism*	解析马克斯·韦伯《新教伦理与资本主义精神》	社会学
An Analysis of Jane Jacobs's *The Death and Life of Great American Cities*	解析简·雅各布斯《美国大城市的死与生》	社会学
An Analysis of C. Wright Mills's *The Sociological Imagination*	解析C. 赖特·米尔斯《社会学的想象力》	社会学
An Analysis of Robert E. Lucas Jr.'s *Why Doesn't Capital Flow from Rich to Poor Countries?*	解析小罗伯特·E. 卢卡斯《为何资本不从富国流向穷国？》	社会学

An Analysis of Émile Durkheim's *On Suicide*	解析埃米尔·迪尔凯姆《自杀论》	社会学
An Analysis of Eric Hoffer's *The True Believer: Thoughts on the Nature of Mass Movements*	解析埃里克·霍弗《狂热分子：群众运动圣经》	社会学
An Analysis of Jared M. Diamond's *Collapse: How Societies Choose to Fail or Survive*	解析贾雷德·M.戴蒙德《大崩溃：社会如何选择兴亡》	社会学
An Analysis of Michel Foucault's *The History of Sexuality Vol. 1: The Will to Knowledge*	解析米歇尔·福柯《性史（第一卷）：求知意志》	社会学
An Analysis of Michel Foucault's *Discipline and Punish*	解析米歇尔·福柯《规训与惩罚》	社会学
An Analysis of Richard Dawkins's *The Selfish Gene*	解析理查德·道金斯《自私的基因》	社会学
An Analysis of Antonio Gramsci's *Prison Notebooks*	解析安东尼奥·葛兰西《狱中札记》	社会学
An Analysis of Augustine's *Confessions*	解析奥古斯丁《忏悔录》	神学
An Analysis of C. S. Lewis's *The Abolition of Man*	解析C. S.路易斯《人之废》	神学

图书在版编目（CIP）数据

解析亚里士多德《尼各马可伦理学》：汉、英/乔瓦尼·盖勒（Giovanni Gellera），乔恩·汤普森（Jon W. Thompson）著；韩晓龙译.
—上海：上海外语教育出版社，2019
（世界思想宝库钥匙丛书）
ISBN 978-7-5446-5932-1

Ⅰ.①解… Ⅱ.①乔… ②乔… ③韩… Ⅲ.①亚里士多德（Aristotle 前384—前322）—伦理学—研究—汉、英 Ⅳ.①B502.233②B82-091.984

中国版本图书馆CIP数据核字（2019）第131185号

This Chinese-English bilingual edition of *An Analysis of Aristotle's Nicomachean Ethics* is published by arrangement with MACAT International Limited.
Licensed for sale throughout the world.

本书汉英双语版由Macat国际有限公司授权上海外语教育出版社有限公司出版。
供在全世界范围内发行、销售。

图字：09 – 2018 – 549

出版发行：上海外语教育出版社
（上海外国语大学内）　邮编：200083
电　　话：021-65425300（总机）
电子邮箱：bookinfo@sflep.com.cn
网　　址：http://www.sflep.com
责任编辑：孙　玉

印　　刷：上海信老印刷厂
开　　本：890×1240　1/32　印张 6.375　字数 130千字
版　　次：2020年11月第1版　2020年11月第1次印刷
印　　数：2 100 册

书　　号：ISBN 978-7-5446-5932-1
定　　价：30.00 元

本版图书如有印装质量问题，可向本社调换
质量服务热线：4008-213-263　电子邮箱：editorial@sflep.com